A Mom after God's Own Heart

A Mom after God's Own Heart

God's Ever-Present Hand in the Life of a Mom

Alexa Shepard

Copyright © 2016 Alexa Shepard.

www.alexashepard.com

All rights reserved. No part of this book may be used or reproduced by any means, graphic, electronic, or mechanical, including photocopying, recording, taping or by any information storage retrieval system without the written permission of the author except in the case of brief quotations embodied in critical articles and reviews.

Scripture taken from the Holy Bible, NEW INTERNATIONAL VERSION®. Copyright © 1973, 1978, 1984, 2011 by Biblica, Inc. All rights reserved worldwide. Used by permission. NEW INTERNATIONAL VERSION® and NIV® are registered trademarks of Biblica, Inc. Use of either trademark for the offering of goods or services requires the prior written consent of Biblica US, Inc.

WestBow Press books may be ordered through booksellers or by contacting:

WestBow Press
A Division of Thomas Nelson & Zondervan
1663 Liberty Drive
Bloomington, IN 47403
www.westbowpress.com
1 (866) 928-1240

Because of the dynamic nature of the Internet, any web addresses or links contained in this book may have changed since publication and may no longer be valid. The views expressed in this work are solely those of the author and do not necessarily reflect the views of the publisher, and the publisher hereby disclaims any responsibility for them.

ISBN: 978-1-5127-3445-4 (sc)
ISBN: 978-1-5127-3447-8 (hc)
ISBN: 978-1-5127-3446-1 (e)

Library of Congress Control Number: 2016904335

Print information available on the last page.

WestBow Press rev. date: 03/29/2016

For My Children
Most of what I have learned in life
I have learned from you.
The greatest gift has been in experiencing the
unfaltering, unfathomable love of God.

Contents

Prologue ix

I

A Heart Condition 1
Speaking the Language of Love 5
Character vs. Personality 9
Know Your Child's Heart 17

II

Rescuing Our Kids 23
Equip Your Kids 31

III

Prayer Jar 35
Random Acts Angel 37
A Reason to Celebrate 39

IV

Raising Boys 45
Raising Girls 51
Surviving Teenagers 61

V

Things that Go Bump in the Night 71
Letting God Handle the Little Things, and the Big .. 79
When Trouble Comes 85

VI

Single Moms 89
Servant Heart 95
The People God Puts in Your Path 103
Retreat to the Desert 109

VII

Letting Go 111
Rewards of Grown-Up Kids 115

VIII

Adoption 119
Our Father 123
Epilogue 127

Prologue

God chose imperfect people, people with flaws, to be his chosen ones to do great things. He chose a person with a sordid past to bring an entire Samaritan village to him, a prostitute to rescue the spies in Jericho, a bankrupt widow to care for the prophet Elijah, and a teenage virgin to bear his son. And he chose you to be a mom.

A Mom After God's Own Heart is not book about how to be a perfect mom. I am far from perfect. It is my hope that this book will show my flaws as well as my strengths. Of all the things I have learned, and as God has transformed me through the seasons of motherhood, the most valuable hardest lesson I've learned, is God is more concerned with the condition of our hearts than our mistakes and bad choices.

This book came about through a constant prodding from God. I kept getting this sometimes constant pushing from God to write about raising my children. I did not understand. I was not a writer; nor did I want to be. Ask me to paint something or write a song, okay, I get that, but a book? What? But God kept at me. I tried for a long time to still the voice inside me, but eventually I said, "Okay, God, I will obey."

This prompting from God came at a low time in my life. I was feeling so defeated. I wanted something more in my life. I was struggling financially. I had aging parents to tend to and teenagers. My art, which was my passion, was not taking off. I felt God was not helping me, or worse yet, I was missing what I was supposed to do. I was crying out, "Less of me, God, more of you," because deep inside I was breaking apart. "God, why have you left me here? Why won't you rescue me?" I hated feeling sorry for myself, but there I was.

As I started to write, something quite unexpected happened. I could see very clearly all the times God had his hand in my life. I could see in black and white all the blessings he provided. I also saw what a wonderful life I had! But the biggest thing of all was I started to see patterns in my life. Things God was trying to teach me and how, through the years, I failed to learn. I realized that the book was for me to share my story. It was not a big career move; it was simply to share God's ever-present hand in the life of a mom after God's own heart.

A Heart Condition

Growing up in a Christ-centered home and spending every Sunday in Sunday school, I knew all the Bible stories. There were two stories I could not wrap my head around and carried into adulthood. I took Bible studies and women's group studies on them, but I could not—and if I'm honest, *would* not—accept them.

The first one was the story of Mary and Martha. Mary and Martha were sisters, and in this particular story, Martha invited Jesus and the disciples over for dinner. Martha was busy. I imagine she was running all through the house, hiding dirty dishes, picking up, sweeping up, and clearing off the table, all while cooking something acceptable for Jesus. During this time, however, Mary sat chitchatting with Jesus. When Martha couldn't take it anymore, she blurted out in frustration to Jesus. Of course Jesus understood and could see how unfair and mistreated she was. But Jesus's response was astounding to me. He told her that Mary had made the better choice! I pictured Martha as the virtuous woman. How could this be? I could relate to Martha.

As a mom, I feel as if I have to be able to do it all. Moms' jobs are nonstop and sometimes inconvenient. At times, I have been called to cook dinner, nurse the baby, help the older kids with homework, and mediate a dispute between the kids—all at the same time. I don't know about you, but if there is another able-bodied adult family member just sitting there doing nothing, I'm probably going to a have a problem with that. And if Jesus were there, I would have thought he would have said, "Hey, get up, and help her out. Can't you see she's doing everything?" But here is what I missed for years.

God is not concerned with how many hats I can wear or how great my performance is. He cares about my heart. Do I have a heart for him? Does he come first? Is he more important than my status, my deeds, and my appearance? And as a mom, am I truly concerned with raising God-loving children, or am I focused on buying more things, keeping up appearances, or keeping the house beautiful?

The second Bible story that I could not understand was the story of King David and Bathsheba. King David sees a woman bathing on the rooftop, and instead of turning away, he watches her and lusts after her. She is beautiful, and he wants her. He is the king, after all, so he sends for her. She is another man's wife. Her husband is fighting a war for the king. After David gets Bathsheba pregnant, he orders her husband to the front lines to be killed. What?

Here is the problem I have. David was God's favorite. He was chosen by God. I read the story and thought, *How can God love him so much?* I don't even like this man; he stole another man's wife, hid it, and then had her husband killed. So why in the world would God favor him? The answer is clear. God saw David's heart, not just his mistakes. David was eventually confronted with his sin and was heartbroken and ashamed—not unlike most of us. We are all prone to human sins; Adam and Eve set that in motion in the beginning. We all mess up and fall into sins, but God is more concerned with our heart condition. And that is the best news!

I didn't understand this until I found myself at the lowest, most broken point in my life. Then this story leaped into my heart, and a flood of tears ran down my face. No matter what I have done, the mistakes I have made, God sees my heart. My heart is for God, and he loves me! I am not a perfect mom. In fact, there have been times in my life when I have made mistakes and bad choices. Unfortunately, some of those choices have affected my children. I will make mistakes. But I am a woman after God's own heart.

> Love the Lord your God with all your heart and with all you soul and with all your strength. These commandments that I give you today are to be upon your hearts. Impress them on your children. Talk about them when you sit at home and when you walk along the road, when you lie down and when you get up. (Deuteronomy 6:5–7)

SPEAKING THE LANGUAGE OF LOVE

How can children grow up in the same home, be raised by the same parents in the same environment and circumstances, and be given the same affection but one of those children feels unloved? I think the answer is that the child's love language was not spoken. Gary Chapman has a great book called *The Five Love Languages*. In the book, he describes how we all give love and feel love in return based on five needs. Those five are gifts, acts of service, quality time, touch, and words of affirmation. We tend to feel loved when we receive love in the form that is our natural inclination.

One of my five children's love languages is gifts. You may tend to think that all children's love language is gifts, but his actions clearly made me realize that he gave love through gifts and felt most loved and valued when given a gift.

When he was very small, he would take out his pacifier and give it to me. When I gave it back, he would be giddy with joy. As he grew into a toddler, he would wrap anything up in paper, Kleenex, socks, or towels and present them to me with such excitement to watch me open them. Sometimes it was a wadded up piece of paper! He would leave me notes to find, and he would talk for weeks about what he wanted to give his brothers and sister for their birthdays. He would count the presents under the tree to see who got the most. In his mind, he believed that the person who received the most was the most loved. Even to this day, I always make sure the presents under the tree are even—or that he gets one extra. As a teenager, he loves to do the grocery shopping and always picks out a little something for a friend who has a birthday—or just because he just knows that person would like it.

Sometimes it's not so easy to tell your child's love language. With my oldest son, I wasn't sure. Nothing jumped out at me to tell me how he felt loved. So I did a test. Every day for one week I spoke one love language. I hugged him and held his hand and gave him high fives. The next week I included him in my errands and sat with him and played video games with him. This I did with each of the five love languages. It allowed me to see how he responded to each. I eventually found out his love language was words of affirmation.

My youngest daughter, as she entered her teenage years, began to cry out her need for quality time with me. Even as I heard her crying out, it was so hard to get off the hamster wheel of working to provide basic food and shelter for my family and run a household that I missed what she was saying. If we listen to what our kids tell us, we can hear when their love language is not being spoken. Kids can also have a secondary love language. In fact, in my experience, I have found that most people have a secondary love language. At certain times in our lives, it can become the dominant language.

We tend to show love to people in our own love language. But if we fail to meet their love language, we end up casting out seed to the wind. If you're still unsure of your children's love language, watch them and see how they express love to others. This is true in our adult relationships as well. We need to know our children. We need to know them deeply enough to know what their hearts need. A mom after God's own heart speaks her child's love language.

Character vs. Personality

A gentle and godly character is not determined by chance or good fortune. It is the result of consistent effort in virtuous thinking and the continued pursuit of godlike thoughts. As a mom, I can tell you that instilling godly character does not happen by accident. It takes purposeful effort on our part to instruct, model, teach, and nurture these traits.

When my children were very little, I wanted to help them develop godly character traits. My firstborn was an angel. He was the perfect child and never disobeyed. If he even thought about doing something wrong, he disciplined himself. One day I saw him sitting in his chair facing the corner. I asked him why he was there. He said, "I thought about taking a cookie after you said no more." He never got dirty or made a mess. In fact, for his first birthday, when the cake was presented to him, instead of using his fingers or diving face-first into the cake, he reached across the table, got a fork, and used that. So you can imagine that I thought I was the bomb as far as being the perfect mom! I marveled at how easy parenting was. I would see other moms and their disobedient children and think, *Wow, they don't have a clue how to raise a child.*

But God has a great sense of humor, and when my second child was born, I know God smiled and gave me a huge dose of humility. My daughter was extremely strong-willed and high energy; she was the life of the party and the center of attention. In fact, when she was born and I heard her first cry, I asked if it was a boy or girl. The doctor replied, "We don't know yet. The baby's not all the way out!" And that's exactly how it went with her. She laughed with everything she had and she cried with everything she had. She was a ball of fiery passion, and she is to this day.

My daughter would never sit in the stroller or in the grocery cart. When I took my two children to the grocery store, I would tell them to put one hand on the cart at all times. My firstborn would hold fast to the cart, but my daughter was quick to let go. When I told her to put her hand back on, she would smile her giddy smile and run the opposite way, laughing all the time. And so, yes, not only did I have my hands full, but I had a heavy dose of humility and shame for all the times I thought I was better than the other moms with disobedient children. God leveled the playing field and humbled my heart.

I decided I needed a new game plan. I needed reinforcements. I starting reading books about "the strong-willed child," and I realized something. I could not change my children's personalities; it was what they were born with and how they were wired. I could, however, help them develop their characters. To me it wasn't enough that my kids would just simply obey me out of fear of punishment or loyalty. I wanted them to actually develop the character traits that made them want to do the right thing. I found two books that emphasized virtues and godly character. When a discipline situation came up, I would sit them in my lap and read to them what God said about what they had done. The book had a Scripture verse and story in language they could understand that talked about mean words, cheating, or stealing. I also used Scripture references from these books to help develop and support our family rules. Two of my favorite books were by author Kenneth Taylor, *Wise Words* and *Children's Book of Virtues*.

I printed a list and hung it on the fridge with things we would honor and things we would not do. We had animals, so I wanted to emphasize how we treat and take care of them. I listed the words from the Anglican hymn "All Things Bright and Beautiful": "All creatures great and small ... the Lord God Made Them All." Beside that I put feed and water and act kind to our dogs. I couldn't stand to hear other children, or adults for that matter, call each other stupid, dumb, idiot, or tell them to shut up. With that in mind, I added that to the list with, "'Reckless words pierce like a sword, but the tongue of the wise brings healing.' Proverbs 12:18." Years later, my middle child told me that he was in sixth grade before he realized "stupid," "idiot," and "shut up" were not real swear words!

One of the most important things you can do is to know your children. Not just their favorite colors, favorite foods, or stuffed animals, but to know them so well you know their weaknesses.

My fourth child was shy and quiet. He was a beautiful child. I mean gorgeous. He was always turning heads with his blond hair and striking lapis-blue pools of eyes. Because he was so shy, he hated any attention. People would stop us everywhere and try to talk to him. His response became to stick his tongue out, or worse! Standing in the grocery line, I would pray no one would talk to us; it was that bad. He was often misunderstood. I understood him so completely, but outsiders would lump him into the category of naughty children. He was incredibly sensitive, and that sensitivity almost always surfaced as anger. I couldn't discipline him like the other children. I would spank him, scold him, and talk with him, but what I got in return was a defiant, angry child. I remember talking to a friend and sharing how completely frustrated I was with him. Her response caught me off guard. She said, "If that was my child, I'd hang myself." Boy did that hurt.

Things got better when I had my fifth baby. My son was so happy and was thrilled that the baby would attract the attention instead of him. I planned a big fiftieth anniversary party for my parents. Over two hundred people were going to attend, including all my parents' close friends and relatives from out of town. I was concerned that my relatives would be all over my son and that it wouldn't turn out well. The week before the big event, I simply said to my three-year-old son, "People are going to come up to you. They are going to talk to you. You do not have to say anything, but you *cannot* spit on them, stick your tongue out, or kick them." After the party, my mom told me that some people had commented my son was so antisocial. They made a big deal about it. I replied, "Mom, did he stick his tongue out at them? Did he spit on them? Did he kick them? No? Then he did just great!"

But deep down I knew I really needed to do heart surgery on his character. I didn't know what to do at first, but I knew I wanted him to develop some godly traits. I suppose I started, like God, at the beginning with creation. I'm not sure why I started there, but looking back at this very moment, it's like a puzzle piece being dropped into place. God led me there to the beginning. We made a trip to the hardware store and bought seeds. We dug up the hard Arizona dirt and planted a garden. We watered, pulled the weeds, and watched it grow. I realized that a child's heart is like a garden. Left neglected or uncultivated, it can run wild. If no useful seeds are put into them, an abundance of weeds will continue to produce their kind.

We started planting rosebushes in our yard, honoring the people we loved in our life. A lavender rosebush reminded me of my grandmother because she had them on her farm. Another was for my children's great-grandmother, who was still alive and meant the world to my kids. As we walked around the yard and watered, pruned, or picked the beautiful flowers, we talked about that person and prayed for him or her.

My son loved picking the vegetables and eating them. To this day he loves vegetables and salads! He learned to be patient by waiting until the vegetables were ready. Sometimes, this was especially hard as our dog loved tomatoes, and on the exact day the tomatoes turned red, our dog would eat them off the vine. We planted carrots and watered them and watered them and watered them.

If you have ever grown carrots, you know how slowly they grow. One day I went outside to find my son. I saw him sitting in the garden with a bag of baby carrots from the fridge, placing them in the ground in perfect little rows. I took a picture and laughed all day about it. He explained it was taking too long for the carrots to grow. I think about that from time to time. How much we are like that in our own lives. Sometimes it seems God is taking too long, so we rush the process along only to find that our actions can never really bear fruit.

My children have taught me that all of us are unique. And where children are concerned, sometimes we have to approach things differently. When my son did something wrong, I sent him directly to his room. I told him when he was ready to talk about it, to call me. Sometimes it would take an hour; sometimes more. As he got older, the time got less. But in those early years, he would be angry in his room for a long time! Eventually, his door would open, and I would hear him call, "Mom, I'm ready to talk." And so we would. He had to have a contrite heart. Only then was his heart open to instruction. He had needed that time to get past his anger and think about his actions. He was a different child when he called me to his room. If he was upset about something, you could not confront him until he was ready. He had a hard time saying he was sorry. In fact, he wouldn't do it even when I knew his heart was repentant, and I knew he felt it. So I came up with a substitute word. A code word he could say that stood for sorry. Eventually he outgrew that code word.

It makes me think of the saying, "You can lead a horse to water, but you can't make him drink." I wanted my children to want to drink! It wasn't enough that they knew godly character. I wanted them to want to have it. A mom after God's own heart knows her children's weaknesses and helps them develop godly character traits.

Know Your Child's Heart

I love my kids with all my heart. I want them to feel safe, happy, and secure, but most of all loved. "And now these three remain: faith, hope and love, but the greatest of these is love" (1 Corinthians 13:13).

I stumbled on a video that was made when my firstborn was a baby. In the video I am clearly having a conversation with my son, and I understand perfectly every word he is saying. I sit there amazed because now, watching this video twenty-four years later, it is as if he is speaking a foreign language. I am touched so deeply that I was so connected to my child that I understood his own language. I believe that is what our heavenly Father is like. He understands our garbled language because he knows our hearts so deeply and is so in tune to us.

When my oldest daughter was very small, we took a trip to our hometown to visit family. My mom and I, with my two small children in tow, went to a fabric warehouse that sold fabric by the pound. This place was a maze. It had boxes of fabric, fur, and trim of every kind stacked to the ceilings with no rhyme or reason to the organization. On leaving the store and putting my children into their car seats, my daughter started crying for her stuffed bunny she had named Bun. My mom and I looked at each other horror-struck. Bun had accompanied us into the store but had not come out. My daughter could not sleep without her Bun. We simply could not leave without it. We searched and searched through the maze of material until finally we found her. I believe God is like that. He knows how much we need him, and he will seek us, no matter how lost we are, because he knows that we cannot live without him. He is our loving Father, who would turn the world upside down, never give up on a lost cause, and is our security.

As a mom, do I focus on the person my child is or on all the things I am doing? When I look at them, do I really see them? Jesus really saw people. When he encountered someone, he saw their needs. They became his priority. He even saw the invisible ones when everyone else overlooked them, such as the poor woman who gave two coins. When everyone else saw the rich put their gifts into the temple treasury, Jesus saw the woman who was very poor put in all the money she had to live on. As moms, we need to open our eyes and truly see those around us. It means setting aside our own agendas for a moment.

When my firstborn was in second grade, the school wanted to advance him two grades. They said he was extremely smart and thought he needed to be in a higher-stimulated class. I prayed about it, and after some long consideration, I told them no. Perhaps my son was highly intelligent, but I knew he was emotionally very young. After all, he was a preschool dropout after two weeks. He lacked the social skills of older kids, and

I knew pursuing intellect over social growth would not make a balanced child. A great teacher gave me a book about the gifted child. I had always hated that word "gifted." All the extremely bright kids I knew lacked common sense. So I was somewhat rebelling against the idea that my own son was gifted. As I read the book, things became clear to me. Extremely bright children are very moralistic, see things in black and white, are perfectionists, and are usually gifted in music and liberal arts. Well, that was my son!

I used to joke that in heaven before my oldest son was born, he got in every line to receive his gifts. He was a genius, charismatic, musically gifted, art gifted, and good-looking. One may say he had it all. But it made his heart very self-reliant, leaving his need for God very diminished. When he was a teenager, he would stand at the top of the stairs when it was time for church and declare he wasn't going. He said he didn't need God; he had a perfect life. I will never forget the day that I told him, "You did not earn your good looks, your musical talent, or your high intellect. These were gifts from God. Someday you will come to the end of your own strength, and God will be the answer." I knew that we never realize God is all we need until God is all we have. That time did come for him when I went through a divorce.

From the very beginning of my first pregnancy, I started journals for my unborn babies. I shared with them how much they were wanted and how excited we were as we anticipated their arrival. I continued to write in their journals through their babyhoods, sharing my thoughts and introspection. When my children graduated high school, I presented them with the journal I had kept so close to my heart. When my oldest son read his journals, he was amazed to see that although I had never spoken it out loud, I had written that I believed he would become a man who served God. I knew my children's hearts. I saw the unique ways in which God had created them. Each one of them was different, and each one of them had their own special attributes.

One day when my youngest son was out in the backyard, he found a baby sparrow fallen from the tree. He wanted to take care of it and make it better. His dad took the bird, threw it over the back fence into the desert, and said, "It won't survive." My son came to me, sobbing for that poor little bird. I knew the chance of that little bird surviving was slim, but I knew with my son's tender heart he needed to try. We found a birdcage the boys had used as a jail for their "fighting guys" and rescued the bird a second time from the desert. My son was four, and neither of us knew how to take care of a baby bird. But my son sat with him bundled up in a towel, sang to him, and loved him. He named him Sparrow. Sparrow lived for four days and died while we were at a school open house. My little boy was devastated.

It wasn't long after that a neighbor offered him a hand-raised baby parakeet. My son was in love. He named him Robin. That bird was my son's best friend. The bird sat on his shoulder all day long. They did everything together. Somehow we ended up with another parakeet, and one day we found an egg in the bird cage. I read up on parakeets, bought a nesting box, and soon we had a whole nest full of baby parakeets. The trick with parakeets, if you want them to like people, is to take over the mama bird's job and hand-feed them. And so we did. Every two hours I or my four-year-old son fed the baby birds. My son developed a deep connection with animals. We had tragedies, of course. My daughter sat on one, and one hit the large picture window when we forgot to clip its wings.

My son rescued a pigeon that had injured its leg. He named it Flamingo and kept it his room in a soda can flat box. That silly bird knew it had it good and never left that box, even though it was only two inches high. My son would take him outside and exercise him. That bird always came back to my son's lap. It was crazy! After some time, Flamingo flew away, but from time to time we would see him.

Eventually, his first beloved parakeet, Robin, died. I took him to the pet store to see the parakeets. He wanted to hold one, but these were "wild" parakeets. They were afraid of people, and when the man opened the cage, the bird flew wildly around the store. Everyone tried to catch the bird, but just when we would get close, it would fly away. Then we looked over and there was that bird perched on my son's tiny finger. The next day, my oldest son and I bought that bird for him. Thunder was always a wild bird, but my son loved it. There have been many other bird rescues through the years.

Eventually we bred American Eskimo dogs, and my son went on to have desert turtles, reptiles, and snakes. I have never been a fan of snakes, but more than that, the only animal that I can't take is rats! And yep, snakes eat rats! Knowing my son had a passion for animals, through the years I have supported his animal ownerships. It was his God-given gift, and I was to nurture and support his gifts.

I was not a fan of the snake idea, but he was fifteen, and he could handle the responsibility with my involvement. Or so I thought. That was until this baby ball python would not eat after we brought him home. After weeks of trying, my son was depleted and devastated. So I stepped in, dangling this dead, thawed mouse on tongs in front of the snake. After a long time, and my arms were about to fall off from fatigue, the snake leaped at it and swallowed it. Remember my fear of rats? Yep, I screamed and ran flailing out of the room, throwing the tongs. After I recovered enough to speak, I told my son, "Don't ever doubt my incredible, endless love for you. I just did that for you!"

My little boy, whom I tended a garden with and allowed to explore his compassion for animals, is registering for college next year in zoology and botany.

Being a mom is not always comfortable, but being a mom and loving your child will allow you to do things you never thought you were capable of. "I can do all things through Christ that strengthens me" (Philippians 4:13).

Rescuing Our Kids

When we rescue our kids from every situation, we are robbing our children of life skills, of overcoming obstacles, perseverance, endurance, and developing godly character traits. If you pray for patience, watch out because God is going to give you opportunities to practice, build endurance, and figure out how to have it. Rarely is a person just born a concert pianist. They practice and practice to achieve mastery.

I have prayed about and for many things, but I have never prayed for my children not to struggle with anything. It is not because I am mean-spirited; it's because I want them to develop mastery when they are little, so when they are older and the situations are much bigger, they will have the tools to overcome them.

When we rescue our kids too soon, we rob them of developing self-confidence. Essentially we are saying, "You're not smart enough, strong enough, or capable of handling this, so I need to step in and take care of it." This is not to say that we should let our kids flail through their problems. We are there to guide them, encourage them, and cheer them on. The hardest thing to do is to know when to lay down your sword and when to pick it up.

I had a simple strategy that helped me identify which was which. When my children were small, as all children, they loved to tattle on each other. It could be very tiresome to hear all of their injustices in a day. So my simple response was, "Is someone hurt? Could someone potentially get hurt?" The joke in our house was, "Are you bleeding? No? Then you're fine." In fact, when one of my boys was learning to drive, he took a corner too fast and too hard. My daughter and I looked at each other with terrorized faces. I started to say something, and my son quickly cut in and said, "Are you bleeding? No? Then you're fine." We burst out laughing. This same strategy has helped me to identify when my teenagers may need me to step in and take charge. Could they hurt themselves or hurt someone else?

With five kids going through the same elementary school, I was involved in the school for sixteen years. So I pretty much knew all the teachers, and there was always a good chance that some of my kids would have the same teachers coming up through the ranks. Sometimes this was a good thing; sometimes I wasn't as excited. But every year toward the approach of school, I prayed for my children's teachers. The prayer would always go like this: "Lord, as the decisions are being made for who will be my children's teachers this year, I pray that you will have your hand in it. Give my children the teachers who will be the best ones to help them develop their godly characters and grow them into the persons you want them to be. I trust you completely."

Of course, when the teachers list would come out and my children heard from their siblings or someone else that he or she had gotten the "mean" teacher, they begged me to switch them out. "But, Mom, all my friends' moms are getting them switched!" But I had a secret weapon. I knew God had chosen that teacher for a reason. However, sometimes it was hard to stand by God's truth.

One of those times was when my oldest daughter got a sixth-grade teacher I didn't know. She was new to the school. As the year progressed, my daughter told me things the teacher had said to her. My daughter was in the honors program, which meant she took math and English in a different room. The teachers were to teach those subjects while the honors kids were in the other class, so the kids wouldn't miss anything. But this teacher was consistently teaching the other subjects while the honors kids were away. My daughter was struggling to keep up on the homework, as most times she didn't know there was any or didn't get the handout. I counseled my daughter to talk with the teacher and explain the situation. The next day when she raised her hand and asked the teacher a question regarding something they had gone over in class while she was in honors, the teacher replied, "Oh look, little Miss Smarty-Pants has a question! Guess she's not as smart as she thinks" I could hardly believe my daughter when she told me.

The next day I bumped into another teacher at school. She pulled me aside and said that she had witnessed my daughter's teacher saying these things to her. *Okay,* I thought, *it's time to step in.* I spoke with the principal, along with the teacher who witnessed these outbursts and told them they needed to stop. The rest of the year got somewhat better, but my daughter never did enjoy that teacher. She muddled through the year just trying to make it work. I wondered, *God, what was good about that experience? What was positive?* All I could think was that life is messy and imperfect. Someday our children will grow up, and they will have a boss who isn't fair and not always nice, and they will have to navigate around it and make it work. Imagine my surprise when eight years later, my youngest daughter got her as her teacher. Oh how I wanted to rescue her. But I stood by God's decision. Would you believe that this teacher was a completely different woman? My daughter blossomed in her class, and it was a good year.

The opposite situation happened with my two middle boys. My younger son got a teacher his older brother had previously had. At the first parent-teacher conference—which, by the way, I will never understand why the kids come with you these days—the teacher, in front of my child, said the most horrible thing. We sat down across from her, and she said, "I was so excited to see I had another Shepard in my class! And then I got him. He's nothing like his brother, but I'm sure he will grow on me."

Imagine my shock! My son's face just sank. When I recovered enough to speak, I said, "No, he's not like his brother. In fact, all his siblings are different. But he has his own strengths and loving qualities." I felt like I had been punched in the gut. I left feeling angry, and the last thing I wanted to do was accept God's plan to have my son in her room all year! Throughout that year it was always something with her. But it allowed us an opportunity for my son and me to talk about things. We learned she had a low self-image and was intimidated easily. She lacked confidence and allowed her personal life to affect her actions. I also learned she was a Christian, and I tried to share my faith with her. I realized then that hurt people hurt people, Christian or not. My son learned a lot about people that year. He learned that even adults can have problems and hurts they carry with them. He learned to not look at the behavior but feel mercy for others. He learned compassion. Why is it that we sometimes believe we know what's best for our kids over God?

When I was a kid we played outside. We were gone for hours. We had no cell phones. We were told to come home when the streetlights came on. We had adventures; we got into trouble, and we had consequences. Nowadays it seems we want to protect our children from consequences. But we need to let them get through it. God does.

I believe kids today are way too micromanaged. Everywhere they go they are supervised by an adult. They don't get to make their own choices. And if they do and it's the wrong one, an adult is there to micromanage the situation, so there are never any natural consequences.

One day I went to pick up one of my boys from middle school. The vice principal met me in the parking lot and told me my son had been hit by another boy and was in the office. I knew what this was about. My son had told me for weeks that another boy was bullying him. I'm a mother, a woman. I have a gentle heart and a nurturing spirit. I don't like fighting and confrontation; I am a peacemaker. I am a woman, after all; God created me this way. So when my son told me about this kid, I told him to walk away. Stay away. Turn the other cheek.

I found my son in the office, blood running down his face, his nose purple and black, and tears streaming down his cheeks. This had happened at the end of the day, and the other boy had gone home. My son told us what had happened. He was leaving the classroom, and another boy was waiting in the hall. As soon as my son entered the hall, this other kid punched him in the nose, blindsiding him. My son tried to kick him away.

We were told to come back in the morning when we would talk more about the situation. The next morning we arrived and waited. I saw the other child and his parents leave the principal's office and go out the front door. I thought, "Good, he is being suspended for his actions." It was our turn in the principal's office. Nothing could have prepared me for what came next. The vice principal told us the other family explained that our son was the real bully and had been picking on this kid for weeks. I was shocked, and anger boiled beneath my skin. Finally, I instructed my child to lift his shirt and pant legs to expose the black and blue marks and scrapes from my son being slammed along the stucco walls. My son was suspended. Because my son openly admitted to trying to kick the other boy, he was equal in fighting. The school's no tolerance to bullying meant that both kids were suspended regardless of the situation. I was bewildered and outraged. Perhaps I had not given my son the best advice.

No one saw my son as the bigger person. He continued to be labeled for the rest of the school year as a wimp, all because I had given him the advice only a mother could give. My son needed advice from a man.

I learned that as much as I wanted my boys to be tender and of godly character, I missed one of the very basic traits of manhood. I missed the warrior. Jesus was a peaceful man, but he, too, had righteous anger when he turned over the tables of the money changers.

That day was an important one for me in parenting. I had lived for years believing that I could be the mother and the father to my children. When I was married, my husband was frequently working or out of town. The kids would tell me from time to time how much they wished their father was more available for them. This made me try even harder to make up for it. I thought that I could wear both hats, and that would be enough. That day in the principal's office I realized I was not equipped to be the dad. God created me, woman, with all the beautiful attributes and character, but not the same ones he created in man.

When one of my boys was in sixth grade, my oldest daughter and I took in cupcakes at the end of the day to celebrate his birthday with his class. The teacher instructed us they had to do one thing before we could give out the treats. We sat patiently in the back of the room. The teacher asked the kids to raise their hand if someone had done something wrong to them today. Hands went up everywhere. As the kids were called on, we heard, "Johnny took cuts in front of me," and "Mary took my pencil." The complaints went on for a full fifteen minutes. My daughter and I just stared at each other, our mouths agape. "Is this tattletale hour?" my daughter asked me in hush tones.

I asked the teacher about it later, and she told me it was part of a state program called "make your day." For days after this incident, I couldn't shake that experience. I finally made an appointment with the principal to discuss this. I felt as if we were robbing our children of developing problem-solving skills. Not to mention giving our children entitlement syndrome, teaching them the misbelief that life is fair, and any injustice to them makes them a helpless victim. I also believe that it makes a disconnection with the kids between each other. It was only focusing on the negative, thus making the whole classroom an unsafe and negative environment. I asked her why the focus was not on the positive things that they saw someone do. This would build the kids up, forge and encourage friendships, and model good behavior. By constantly pitting the kids against each other, they were dividing the children instead of bonding them. We adults need to be careful not to micromanage our children. When we do, we rob them of developing very important skills they will need to navigate through life. Though the principal agreed with me, unfortunately, it was a state program and would remain in the classroom.

Equip Your Kids

I have always felt very blessed to have had parents who were born during the Depression and grew up in large, farm families. Because of that, my parents taught me to waste nothing, and never pay to have something done that I could do myself.

We live in a world of overflowing landfills, and everything is disposable. I run into people who are crippled in everyday life by lack of knowledge or the ability to figure things out. As a child, I thought my dad could make or fix anything. When I got older, I still thought my dad could make or fix anything. My dad is eighty-four now, and I realize he can make or fix anything! My mom could look in an almost empty cupboard and come up with a feast. I didn't realize it at the time, but my parents were teaching me and passing down life skills I would use throughout my life.

In today's generation, we have so many fractured families. Generations and families are spread throughout the country. Traditions and crafts are not passed down like they used to be. With so many dual-career families, there is little time to do, let alone teach, crafts and skills. I don't know how many people I know say they don't know how to make gravy. It's one of the easiest things to make from scratch, but no one ever showed them.

I was passionate about teaching my children many things. I wanted to equip my kids to be able to succeed and thrive in life. I watched a fascinating PBS program called *Frontier House*. They took modern families and placed them in Montana to see if they could have survived a winter in the 1800s. With no electricity or modern technology, these families were left with making a life using their skills. It was riveting to see what they were capable of, and it made me wonder, *Have I taught my children the skills to survive without the luxury of modern technology and the Yellow Pages? Have I taught them the simple things like sewing a button on, hemming pants, and how to use a sewing machine?"* These things were the basics that everyone should know.

My grandmother taught me to knit, but my sister is excellent at it and has taught both my girls to knit. My dad was notorious for thinking outside the box. Remember that show *MacGyver*? That was my dad. I picked this up through the years, and I am passing this down to my children, fixing broken appliances, a part on the car, or using everyday things to get the job done instead of buying an expensive fix. For a few years we lived on a cul-de-sac with a great big backyard. Part of it was fenced off, and my dad used to work on cars or fix things back there. We called it the junkyard. He used to come over early in the morning and start his projects. Many mornings we would wake up and everyone would be looking for my middle son, who was about two years old at the time. We'd say, "Go look in the junkyard." Sure enough, sometimes in his pajamas or just his underwear, there he was, squatting to watch his grandfather work on something. Maybe my son will never be a mechanic or excel at rebuilding things, but those moments taught him something else. He saw "man in motion." He learned what tools were which. And he learned that Grandpa can fix anything.

I am an artist. I create things. In fact, the kids joke that if something sits still long enough, Mom is going to paint it. I dabble in every craft imaginable. So it should be no surprise to me when I come home and find my children making, creating, and designing things. But oh, the mess! I think in surprise, *Why do they feel the need to start a project at nine thirty at night and create all this mess?* Then I take a long look in the mirror and think, *Ah, my greatest creations.*

If you don't have many skills or talents, find someone who does to teach your children. As a mom, I believe it's our job to expose our children to many things so that when the time comes, they can sift through their vast experiences and know what they are passionate about. There is nothing worse than a God-given talent that is never uncovered. I understand that not all people are crafty and creative. But this was my gift from God, and I am using it. Whatever your gift, use it and pass it down to your children. When we are truly doing what we were designed to do, it fills all the empty spaces with love.

Prayer Jar

To encourage my children to pray, I made a prayer jar. I took a big kitchen jar, and we wrote the names of people in our lives on pieces of paper. The names included the children's teachers, principal, Sunday school teachers, the president of the United States, their friends, and family members. This jar sat on our kitchen table, and when it came time to say grace at dinner, the kids begged to be the one to say grace. They picked a slip from the jar, and the person's name that was on it was to be included in their prayer. Two things started to happen. My children, who didn't want to say grace, suddenly were begging for the chance. The second thing was the prayers had thought; they were not just some memorized verse or table grace. But the most amazing thing was hearing a child's heart pray for someone in his or her life. Sometimes the same name was drawn multiple times in that week. This was an amazing thing in and of itself because we had many, many names in the jar. The kids always wanted to redraw, but it was an opportunity to heighten our awareness that maybe this person needed extra prayers.

Alexa Shepard

I felt it was important to teach my children to pray for others. We live in a world where self-reliance and self-promotion abounds. Taking our eyes off ourselves teaches our hearts to develop compassion and empathy for others and their situations.

Random Acts Angel

As my children approached their teenage years, I started to see a disconnection from being kind and doing nice things for each other without a potential gain in mind. I had a beautiful angel ornament and decided it would be a "random acts angel." At one of our family meetings, I announced that the angel was part of our home now.

The rules were that you were to do something kind for someone else, like make the person's bed, fix him or her a treat, or put their brother's or sister's clothes away. You were to leave the angel on the pillow, so he or she knew that a random act of kindness had been performed. You were to do this in secret, so the receiver didn't know who had done it. The point was to do something with no reward for you in it. After receiving the angel, you had three days to give it to someone else.

A Reason to Celebrate

My mom was passionate about decorating for the holidays. Not just the big ones but all the little ones in-between, right down to the color of the tablecloth. As a child I loved it! Coming home from school and seeing the holiday boxes out put a smile on my face and joy in my heart. My sister felt none of this. It is no surprise that I, too, now have my own set of holiday-themed boxes.

I love holidays. Maybe it's just because it's a reason to celebrate in an otherwise day-to-day task of life. It takes our eyes off the everyday and gives us a chance to rejoice. It could possibly be, too, that it marks a changing of seasons. Living in Phoenix, Arizona, we might not know it was spring or fall if we didn't have a calendar.

There is nothing like experiencing Christmas through the eyes of a child. When my oldest son was very small, I took him to sit on Santa's lap. I wanted that classic picture of my child sitting on Santa's lap. My son would have nothing to do with any Santa! I did find it amazing, though, that wherever he saw a nativity scene he would squeal with glee and wanted to go right up to it and touch baby Jesus.

One time we were sitting in church, and they were acting out the nativity story. When they got to the part where the shepherds walked in, my youngest daughter leaned in and whispered in awe, "Were we there?" Having the last name Shepard was confusing, but when they asked the audience for volunteers to be shepherds, my kids raised their hands, "We are shepherds"!

We had a simple manger scene that I loved as a child. My mom gave it to me, and it was a central focus in our home for the holidays. One day my oldest son said, "Mom, why is baby Jesus is in the manger already? He doesn't get born until Christmas." I followed his cue and removed baby Jesus and tucked him safely into my dresser drawer. On Christmas Eve I would retrieve him while we were playing Santa and place him in the manger. It was the first place my son looked on Christmas morning. "Yep, baby Jesus is here." A promise fulfilled. With that I got another idea. If baby Jesus doesn't belong in the manger until Christmas morning, what about the wise men? They traveled far to see the King. I let my children take the three wise men and move them from room to room around house in the days leading up to Christmas. It was their journey to Bethlehem.

The one thing I did not enjoy about Christmas was the endless rushing around to buy gifts. My children always wanted to buy their siblings gifts that I knew would be quickly discarded—along with all my money. I wanted my children to learn to give, not just receive, so I had to come up with something.

I decided that all Christmas gifts had to be handmade or gifts of service. The only gifts that didn't have to be handmade were gifts from Santa. It was one of my best decisions. Instead of just checking off a list, I spent time really thinking about the people I was making gifts for. I made a designated craft night once a week and invited my mom, sister, and friends over to work on their projects. My children, as they got older, sat around the table with us, making jewelry, boxes, or learning to embroider dish towels. It was so much fun to talk about fond memories and pray for the people we were making gifts for. I wanted my kids to know that we give gifts to symbolize God's greatest gift to us: his Son. The wise men came bearing gifts to the would-be King to honor him and worship him.

My children were to give each other gifts that they had made or an act of service for them. Sometimes they made little coupons to redeem for picking up their toys or taking them for a bike ride. Even today, the kids give an act of service for cleaning out their cars or giving them a manicure. It is important to me that each year I make something special for each child. As they have gotten older, it is harder; it takes more thought. But it is a tradition I have built and one I am not ready to give up. There were nights I was up till the crack of dawn, finishing the last shingle on a dollhouse or stitching up the last teddy bear. But these moments only add to the rich memories I have of creating from my hands a gift of thought.

Perhaps my very favorite holiday is Easter. It may be the chocolate bunnies, the chocolate eggs, or the chocolate candy bars. It's hard to decide. The beauty of an Easter basket is something to behold. Okay, I obviously love chocolate. I also love tulips. There is something beyond their beauty that calls to my soul. It's the simple, plain-looking bulb that once a year grows and, with patience, blooms a vibrant, perfect flower. The beauty of the flowers only lasts for a few days and then they are gone. We have to enjoy them in the moment, or we will miss their glory.

My children loved to hunt for Easter eggs. My youngest son loved it the most. For the month before Easter, he would go to his great-grandma's house and practice. She looked forward to their little game of hiding the eggs and him dutifully retrieving them. When she died, we placed an Easter egg with notes from my children, saying how much they loved her and would miss her, where others left flowers. Great-grandma loved Jesus with all her heart, and she loved hunting eggs with the kids.

Because this is such a fond memory for my children, we always hunt Easter eggs no matter how old they are. When they were young, I color-coded the eggs for each of my children. I placed one egg in their baskets so they would know which color they were hunting for. That way the bigger kids would not get all the eggs. As my children got older, I had to step up my game. One year when the kids found their Easter baskets there was a flashlight inside. We hunted Easter eggs in the dark with only our flashlights. Then I got really creative and bought glow-in-the-dark Easter eggs, and we hunted eggs after the sun went down.

But perhaps the biggest reason I love Easter so much is because of the fulfillment of a promise. It is the incredible willingness that Jesus had to lay down his life for us. It is what he taught us from the cross when he said, "Forgive them, for they know not what they do." (Luke 23:34) It is my measuring stick for how to forgive. When all I can think, *God, look what they did to me. How can I forgive?* Jesus shows me his pierced hands and feet and says, "Look what they did to me."

Raising Boys

There is something quite magical between mothers and their little boys. I know so many pregnant women who fear having a boy because they think they won't know quite what to do with them and won't understand them. In truth, it's men we can't figure out!

The bond between a mother and son is critical. You are his first imprint of woman. When you take care of his cuts and scrapes, you are teaching him a woman can be tender. When you tend to the needs of your sick child, you are teaching him a woman can be compassionate. When you listen to your son with your full attention, you are teaching him a woman can be trustworthy. When you teach him about pornography and sex, you are teaching him a woman is valuable. When you don't yell and scream when he breaks something but help him clean it up, you are teaching him a woman can be forgiving. When you tuck him in at night and say prayers with him, you teach him a woman can be safe. I cannot stress enough that it is easier to raise healthy boys than to fix broken men.

Boys are wild and adventurous at heart. They love to build towers just to knock them down. They love forts, splashing in the mud puddles, and firecrackers. The first noise they will make is the vroom, vroom of a car, and they will take their blankies and make a superhero cape. They love campfires and frogs and bugs, which makes them very dangerous! My heart wants to sing when I see little boys at play. They can be brave and fearless and then crawl up into your lap and snuggle close to you. It's that salty and yet sweet that sucks you in.

Little boys are simple and uncomplicated. They don't fabricate stories or embellish things. They just say it like they see it. I started to notice that my son's kindergarten papers were all coming home with the name Bob on it. I thought, *He must have gotten his papers mixed up with another little boy by mistake.* Before long I was down rabbit trail, thinking, *What if they have my son's name wrong? What if they don't have my son on the roster at all? What if he never got registered?* You can see my mind was in overdrive. I took a deep breath and asked my son if they were his papers. He said, "Yes." I asked him why "Bob" was written in the name spot. He said, "My name is too long to write, so I write Bob instead." Simple, uncomplicated, and it made perfect sense to him.

Little boys grow into young men, and their adventures grow with them. My middle son had to write an essay in high school on the scariest thing that ever happened to him. It had to be a true story. When I was cleaning up the kitchen one afternoon, I noticed the essay on the counter. What caught my eye was the red ink written across the paper: "Great story, but the assignment was to write a true story." I was intrigued.

I grabbed my cup of coffee and sat down at the kitchen table and began to read. It read,

> The scariest day of my life was when I was sent to the neighborhood park to tell my younger siblings it was time for dinner. As I was walking on the sidewalk, a car pulled up behind me, and before I knew it, someone was putting a pillowcase over my head. I was thrown in the trunk of the car and driven around. I was so scared. That was until I heard the voices in the car and realized it was my older brother and his friend.

Wow! How could I have not known about that? I asked my son about it later that day, and yes, it was true.

Boys will protect their mom. Moms are sweet and nurturing and kind. Moms wouldn't fit in the rough and tumble world of adolescent boys. I am sure that there are many other things that the boys did not let me catch wind of. I also know that the bond of brotherhood is sacred, and throwing each other under the bus is against their code.

There will come a time when your precious little boy will start to pull away from you. This happens in their early teens, usually around the time they enter middle school. It happens to every mom. At first you don't really recognize the gentle swing away from you, but in time, it is a very real, ever-present void. When my oldest son began to pull away from me, I was scared. It was an actually physical feeling of loss. I soon understood that this is very normal, and it is the way God created boys to be. They start to identify with who they are in the world around them. They venture past their secure little nest and begin to take on the world. In the beginning, they will dip back into their safety pool of Mom only to hunt and explore the world again. It's hard. As a mom, it's hard to let this special bond slip away. But it is necessary to their development into the men they will become. You can choose to hold on to them or be their best cheerleader. Our job—our privilege—is to train, teach, and direct our boys to become healthy, strong, God-loving men. That's our job, plain and simple.

My middle son felt this shift in our relationship himself. He wrote me a letter about how bad he felt about our roles changing. I gently reminded him that it was okay; it is the way it is supposed to be. Boys start to identify more with men and need men more in their lives, men they can emulate and learn how to be a man in the world. The best thing you can do is make sure that they have good male role models in their lives.

It is so important for a boy to have a strong, healthy dad. Unfortunately, this is not a void that a mother can fill no matter how hard we try. I struggle with this for my boys and my girls. It is hard for me to admit that there is something I can't do, a limit to my bag of tricks. But I finally understood that as much as I have tried, I can't give to my children what they need from a father. It broke my heart. Then I realized I could point them to their heavenly Father.

Recently, I walked up to a Circle K convenience store. I arrived at the door at the same time a young man in his thirties did. He motioned "After you," and

I proceeded to open the door. He walked right past me through the door I was holding open. I felt it proved the point I had made the other night—men in our generation have no chivalry. Nor do they have the instinct to protect or defend women. My friend pointed out that all this women's lib and equality of women created this. I disagree. If men would step up and be the men God designed them to be, women would not have to do their jobs, too. When I was leaving Circle K, I was startled by a man in his seventies who came sprinting across the store and announced, "Let me get that for you."

It is up to us to teach our boys manners. It doesn't just happen, and they will not learn them from society. When we teach our boys to develop their God-given attributes, we instill in them much more than good manners. We give them value. God designed man to protect, defend, and rescue woman. Do not deprive them of their God-given desires.

Raising Girls

Raising girls is like Alice falling through the looking glass. Everything can be normal one minute, and then everything can be so different. Little girls have the luxury of straddling two worlds—the rough and tumble of boys and the frilly delicateness of girls.

My oldest daughter was a tomboy. She loved bugs and sword fighting and only wanted to play on the boys' sports team because girls were too girly. She wore red cowboy boots with everything and couldn't sit still long enough to have her hair brushed. I used to have a bathroom drawer full of suckers, and I would sit her on the edge of the sink and give her one while I brushed her hair. It was the only way to keep her sitting still. But we also had tea parties and makeup nights. My daughter grew into a beautiful young woman who went to cosmetology school, wears high heels, and does makeup and up-dos for weddings.

When my youngest child was born, I was so excited to have another girl. I wanted so much for this little girl to be the stereotype everyone said girls were. How amazing it would be to have the baby who sits on the blanket and is quiet and delicate. I guess the genes to have that baby are not in my particular DNA.

My youngest daughter was the last baby to complete our family. Because I knew this, everything about her was magical. From the moment I was pregnant, I savored every detail of my blossoming pregnancy as if it were a fine piece of chocolate or a deep-red, rich glass of wine. I was fascinated by every detail; the ones I seemed to rush past in all my other pregnancies. I know it sounds crazy, but even through labor, I marveled at the miracle that was happening before my very eyes. She was a gift. God had given me so many, but I hadn't stopped long enough to really see that God was in the details.

Girls are complicated. I can say this because I am one. I picture a girl's thought process like a pearl necklace. Each thought is connected to another to make it whole. Snip one pearl away, and the whole thing falls apart.

While boys ask why to everything, girls ask how come. I can't tell you the number of circular conversations I have had with my little girls.

"Mommy, how come the sky is blue?"
"Because God made it that way"
"How come he made it that way?"
"I guess God just likes the color blue."
"How come he made the grass green then?"
"I guess he likes the color green, too."

And it goes on and on until I blatantly change the subject to "Hey look, I saw a kitty." Yeah, there was no cat, but please.

When my oldest daughter was five, we all noticed that her voice was hoarse all the time, and when she talked, it was kind of breathy. We all joked that it was because she never stopped talking. I took her to an ear, nose, and throat doctor who found she had nodules on her vocal chords. You guessed it. It was probably there because she was a nonstop, singing chatterbox. They put her on voice rest. That meant no talking. It almost killed her. It was literally torture to her. Whenever she started to talk, we put our finger to our lips to remind her, and she would burst into tears. It broke my heart and crushed her spirit. She didn't know how to write yet, so she had all these things to communicate and couldn't. The frustration brought her to tears. That's how strong a girl's heart is wired to communicate. It's a perfect example of how we are made. It's no wonder that women who are not allowed to share their feelings and their thoughts simply begin to wither inside.

 Little girls get their value and self-image from their fathers. Sadly, we as moms cannot fill these shoes. Trust me, I have tried. I was so blessed to have a dad who thought I was amazing. It wasn't so much in the words he said to me as it was in his actions. He was at every soccer, softball, basketball, and track event. He sat through every band concert, choir concert, and play I was ever in. He spent time with me and taught me things, even if it was just holding the flashlight or handing him a wrench. After one of my speech and debate tournaments, my parents' friends told me, "Your dad thinks you could be the president of the United States." My dad was proud of me. When I got divorced, my dad put his arm around me and said, "I will love you no matter what." Then, with a big smile on his face to lighten the mood, he said, "Just promise me you won't marry a twenty-year-old." My dad accepted me. His love was not conditional.

My husband, on the other hand, worked a lot. He was often busy at work and not able to come to the kid's concerts, award ceremonies, and plays. My youngest daughter really struggled and, honestly, still struggles with this. I tell her that her father loves her very much. I tell her it is not a reflection of how he feels about her or how special she is to him. I also let her know that it makes me sad that she feels this way. I try to point her to the fact that although her dad cannot always be that for her, she has a grandfather who is. My dad goes to every softball game, even in his eighties in 110 degree weather, and every event—big and small—in her life. My dad will drop everything to pick them up or drop them off somewhere. When my kids stop in unexpectedly to play cards with my parents, my dad's face lights up like the Fourth of July. He thinks they are amazing, beautiful, and perfect.

As great as that is, there is something even more wonderful. We have a heavenly Father who thinks we are perfect. Why? Because he numbered the hairs on our heads. We are the crowns of his creation. He made us perfectly in his image, and he delights in us. That is the true secret to every woman. No matter how old we are. The secret to a woman's self-confidence and value is in Christ. That is what we must give our girls.

When I was thirteen, I got my period. It was horrible, and I cried. It was the worst thing that could happen to a teenage girl who was a sporty tomboy. I was at my sister's house, spending the night before a big soccer game. When I woke, I thought the whole world was unjust and being a girl was terrible. My kind-hearted sister took me to the store to buy pads. You know the ones I'm talking about; the great, big, huge, bulky things that feel like a diaper. I went to the game utterly self-conscious in my tight, little soccer shorts. I didn't want to move, let alone run on the soccer field. But that was not an option. I always played the whole game; I was never on the bench. At halftime, my mom came up to me and asked what was wrong with me. She said I was running like I had a cobb up my butt. Well, I felt like it! I didn't want to tell her I had my period. I didn't want anyone to know. I was embarrassed and ashamed.

So when the time drew near for my oldest daughter to get her first period, I wanted it to be a different experience than I had. I wanted her to embrace it. I wanted her to feel like she was becoming the woman God created her to be. I must have gone overboard on my delivery, because the day my daughter got her period, she sang from the rooftops and wanted to know where we were going for dinner to celebrate.

I love the story of creation. Being an artist, I marvel at the Master Creator and his beautiful depiction of his masterpiece. God created all the heavens and earth, the oceans and the animals, and finally, he created man in his own image. He sat back and looked at all he had created and said, "Something is missing" And then he created woman. Only then did he say it was complete. Woman was created on purpose! We were not a mistake or an afterthought. We were designed to complete God's reflection of his image. Being created in his image means more than a physical likeness. It is his attributes that God reflected. God created girls to be sensitive, to feel things deeply, because God himself does. He made girls complex and mysterious to mirror his attributes.

I want my girls to know, above all else, that our innate value and significance are through God's eyes. It is his opinion of us—not that of a boyfriend or husband—that matters. "I praise you because I am fearfully and wonderfully made" (Psalm 139:14).

Girls believe that the world should be fair. It's almost like we are shocked when people don't play fair, fight fairly, or bad things happen for no good reason. The number of times I have heard my teenage daughter say, "But, Mom, it so unfair," are too numerous to count. And yet it is. But there is a bigger lesson, and I think sometimes God uses it to get our attention and change us. I tell my girls not to expect life to be fair. Others will do and say hurtful things you do not deserve. When others mistreat you, view it as an opportunity to grow in grace. Don't obsess about other people's opinions of you. It is God's opinion of you that matters.

By far the most common words from my daughters' lips are, "But I'm tired of being the bigger person." My response is always the same, and I'm sure they hate that, but our job is to raise God-honoring, God-loving children. I remind them that the only person we have control over is ourselves, and we have a choice to make. We need to be the best person we can be and do what is right, even if the whole world is doing wrong. When my children were little I always asked them, "What would Jesus do?" My son, after he had been reprimanded and asked how he was going to resolve the situation for hitting his sister, said, "Well, Jesus wouldn't have hit her in the first place." I laughed a little on the inside. He got it. Doing what is right is never wrong. It restores our relationship with God, honors the Holy Spirit in us, and fills us with peace.

Every mom wants her daughter to grow up and be cherished by the man in her life. Every girl wants to be loved deeply. She wants to be loved just the way she is. She wants to be enough. God planted in us these desires on purpose. And I want my girls to know that it was not so we would go from relationship to relationship, looking to have that. He made this unquenchable desire in us so that we would turn to him, the only person who could fulfill this longing. You are not crazy or selfish to want these things. You were designed that way!

Having said this to my daughters, I wanted to emphasize that they should be loved by someone special. They should be with someone who is kind, respectful, and values them, but do not look for perfection. No one is perfect, and no one can live up to that expectation. People will let you down from time to time, but God never will. He created you. You are his beautiful masterpiece just the way you are. He loves you just the way you are, faults and all. Do not get your self-worth from other people. Get it from God.

I want my girls to know that they are chosen. They are fearfully and wonderfully made. Never, never, never, will God leave you. He has a purpose, and he will do abundantly more than we could ever ask or think. He gave us the Holy Spirit to be our companion. It is that still, small voice inside of us that alerts us to things that may harm us. All we have to do is listen and not let the broken world around us drown out that voice. These are the blessings we receive from God on a daily basis as he renews our minds and transforms our hearts.

Here's what no one tells you when you bring your little girl home from the hospital. Here's what no one whispers in your ear when your teenage daughter is yelling at you. Just hold on. Hang in there. You will be her number 1 when she is an adult.

I know this because my mom is an irreplaceable part of my life. Even to this day, when I am sick or hurt or need someone to comfort me, I want my mom. When I want the truth, I go to my mom. My mom is honest. Sometimes the things she has to say are painful to hear, but if I'm honest, there is usually some truth in them. As a teenager it was frustrating, but as an adult, it is refreshing. She tells it like she sees it. When no one else has the guts to say the truth, my mom does. My mom doesn't give out false praise or say something just to make me feel better. If she says it, she means it. You always know how she feels and where she stands. There is a great comfort in that; it is exhilarating.

The other day my mom told me that I was the "Proverbs 31" woman. I was touched so deeply. It meant the world to me. She wasn't saying it to make me feel good; she was saying it because she felt that way. If anyone else in the world had said that to me, it would not have even come close to how much it meant coming from my mom.

My mom is a great measuring stick for being true to oneself. She doesn't let things fester and grow into bitterness; she simply states them. My girls will occasionally approach me and ask me if an outfit they are wearing is appropriate. My best defense is to ask, "What would Grandma say?"

They usually reply, "I'll go change." My girls know that Grandma tells it like she sees it. And they also know that sometimes we all need that.

I talk to my mom on the phone almost every day. Sometimes I just need to. I can't explain why, but I need to hear her voice, share my day, and hear about hers. I have noticed this in my oldest daughter, too. She calls me a lot. I talk to her a lot more than my boys. Sometimes she wants comfort; sometimes just to catch up. Girls need their moms. As we get older, our moms are an irreplaceable part of our lives. I want to give my girls what my mom gave me—the painful truth when I have missed the mark and the glorious praise when I hit a home run. I want it to mean something to them.

So when your little girl is a daddy's girl or that teenager yells at you and tells you she doesn't need you, hold on. She will. You will be her number 1 go-to person as she navigates the world, gets married, and raises her own family. Girls need their moms even when they are all grown up.

Surviving Teenagers

Raising teenagers takes courage and is not for wimps. You need to have thick skin and more patience than you can ever imagine. Having had five kids go through the "terrible teenage years," you would think it would be old business for me. But no matter how many kids you raise, having a teenager never gets easier.

My youngest daughter arrived at teenage-dom with full force. One day I'm her favorite, and she's singing, "Mom is the best; she's amazing! I love her," and the next day I'm Satan's field hand. You never know from minute to minute which one you will be in their eyes. On days when I'm at the end of my courage and strength, I call my oldest daughter. I replay my wounded heart and all the injustices I have endured. And my beautiful daughter says, "Mom, you can do this. You are the strongest person I know. You are the greatest mom, and she loves you. Remember, I was like that, too. You've been through this before, and it will pass. Stay the course and you'll get through it." At those times I love her so much I want to cry.

When children are small, it's the physical demands that wear us out and threaten to burn us out. It's the endless piles of laundry and the flu that goes through the house only to be picked up by the first one who had it and the process repeated. The constant holding, bandaging, rocking; reading, carrying around and putting back to bed after a nightmare, the picking up of toys, cleaning up spills, vacuuming, sweeping to get the dirt off the floor from your crawling baby is exhausting.

I was a much better mom to my kids when they were little. The church asked me to take over the youth group. I had no desire to. I didn't like teenagers! But I did it. For one night. Then I begged, "Put me in the two-year-old room. I can't take this!"

My dear friend told me, "You know, one day all five of your kids will be teenagers." Yeah, I wasn't looking forward to that. I am struggling through those teenage years now, and I will tell you, some days I'm just waiting to get through it in one piece.

Although you cannot convince a young mother this, the physical demands of small children are nothing compared to the emotional demands of teenagers. One minute you're telling your toddler, "Don't eat the dog's food," and before you know it, you're telling your kids not to put drugs in their body. The dog food won't kill them, but the drugs might.

My children are about two years apart. I didn't plan it that way; it's just the way it turned out. I always wanted to have eight kids. That was my dream. But it was not my husband's dream. He worked a lot and was out of town a lot, so I was basically raising these children on my own. But what ultimately helped me let go of my dream was the realization that I could not be the same mom I was to my older children that

I was to my younger ones. Five children spanning ten years meant that I would have a toddler and teenager at the same time. That required me to have my head in two places and the physical exhaustion from babies and the emotional roller coaster of teenagers. The vastly different needs they would require and the fear I would not be able to do justice to both released my dream of more children.

Children emulate their parents, whether it's a conscious choice or subconsciously through osmosis. On a recent visit to my parents' house, my mom was talking about how much my dad frustrated her. Specifically frustrating was his easygoing attitude. At first, I defended him, saying that was a good thing. It was secretly something I admired very much. But as she shared she said he avoids conflict and confrontation. He believes things will just workout on their own. My dad chimed in from the other room, "And they almost always do."

"Yes," my mother said, "but you avoid taking action unless it's your idea." Now I was riveted.

This was the exact thing I had been struggling with all week with my boyfriend, and if I'm honest, for the past eight years. I was just like my dad. After I left my parents' house, I really thought about the exchange I had just had with my folks. All my life I had admired my dad. No, that's an understatement. I thought he was amazing and the most God-honoring man I had ever known. I was adopted, so when I saw his reflection in my character, I knew this was not a hereditary trait. I admired him so much that subconsciously, I had become like him. I also learned that what I admired was not always seen as admirable in other people's eyes. What I found most fascinating, though, was that I had embraced something without even realizing it. It was something modeled by my parent. It's not always the things that you set out to teach your children that influence them. More often than not it's the way you live your everyday life.

As my children have been growing to adulthood, they will tell me that phrases I used to say to them over and over when they were little have spilled out of their mouths without thought. When my oldest daughter was little and I told her something, she would always respond, "I know." It had become more of a habit than it was a pride issue. So I would tell her, "To know and not to do is not to know." That became my little mantra to her. One night at work, a coworker kept saying, "I know," to my daughter who was training her on the job. Exhausted and exasperated, she said, "To know and not to do is not to know." Her hand flew to her mouth. "Where did that come from?" When she told me later, we laughed until we were sick.

My youngest daughter was a little rough and aggressive when she was a baby. It was probably because she had four older siblings and had learned to fight for her place. When she shoved or grabbed someone by the cheek when they were frustrating her, my mantra to her was, "Nice hands, nice hands." One day while sitting in her high school class, someone kept pinching her face and pestering her purely out of fun. My daughter said she turned to them and said, "Nice hands, nice hands." Of course, I had to tell her the story of when she was a baby, and we had said that so many times to her. What we put into our children is often a direct result of what will come out, good or bad.

Being a teenager is like being on an on-ramp during rush hour, trying to merge onto the freeway for the first time. Everything we have taught them to this point on is what they will draw from to navigate this world. They will test it. That is why I believe that we must be honest and humble at this stage. Owning up to our own faults, shortcomings, or mistakes builds trust and shows them that we have our eyes wide open.

I make mistakes. My kids know this, and more important, they know that I know it. At times I have said the wrong thing or something unkind out of anger or frustration. I remember saying to my kids many times, "I love you, and you're so important to me. I'm so sorry I just said that or did that. Forgive me." I asked for their forgiveness because I recognized their enormous value to God. I modeled to them that I cared more about honoring them than I did about my pride. It is not their job as children to love you unconditionally. It is your job as a parent to love them unconditionally.

Do not be afraid to talk to your kids about the hard stuff. As my teenagers started to make their own decisions on things, I was there to redirect them on occasion. One day my boys rented a movie from Redbox. I had always been conscious of what movies I watched and exposed my children to. R rated movies are hardly R anymore. When I saw what they were watching, I was appalled. I immediately turned the movie off and told the boys we needed to go for a walk. I explained to my boys what it meant to honor God with our bodies, which included our eyes. I recalled the verse, "Whatever is true, whatever is noble, whatever is right, whatever is pure, whatever is lovely, whatever is admirable—if anything is excellent or praiseworthy—think about such things" (Philippians 4:8). I did not want my boys to become desensitized to things that are not good. More than that, I wanted them to have the value and belief to make God-honoring choices from their own hearts. I am thankful that my oldest son took over that conversation and shared from his heart the dangers that men can fall into if they do not head God's direction on maintaining a pure heart.

I have had many conversations with my boys about pornography. I was cleaning my oldest son's room when he was in middle school and found a Victoria's Secret catalog under his rug. My first thought was to take a magic marker out, draw clothes on all the models, and place it back. I didn't want to embarrass my son for his natural curiosity, but I did want to talk about the hard issue at hand. I started to notice on the computer history log that my son had been visiting porn sites. I sat him down and had a heart to heart with him about porn. I explained to him the highly addictive nature of porn and the devastating effects it has on the lives it touches. I told him that porn objectifies women; it makes them an object for their selfish pleasure and takes away their God-given purpose for intimacy. In fact, porn is void of any intimacy and destroys intimacy with another person. My son wrote me a letter, years later, thanking me for having the courage to talk to him about this. The week before he was married, he came into my room to talk. He told me he had told his bride-to-be that he had been addicted to pornography when he was in high school. My son broke down in tears as he told me how hard it was to see his beautiful fiancée cry.

I have always liked my body. When I look in a mirror, I think, *You look pretty good.* In truth, I probably have the opposite of anorexia, if there is such a thing. People with eating disorders look at their emaciated bodies and see them as fat. The opposite of this is probably close to what I have. I look and see something better than what I am. And I'm okay with that. The problem comes when I look at myself through other people's eyes. I see all my faults and start to dislike my body. At times I have to catch myself making negative comments about my body. As a mom, it is so important to guard negative talk about our bodies from our teenage girls. This is super hard! We joke about our extra weight or stretch marks to fit in. We make wisecracks about it, so no one else says it behind our backs. But what message are our young girls really hearing?

I am five feet two, and a size zero. I am the same size now that I was in high school. My daughters are five feet eight, and a few sizes bigger than me. If I complain about my body and size, what message am I sending them? They may not have inherited my body type, but they can inherit my positive self-image.

Teenage boys and girls can, and usually will, gain weight. It usually hits them in middle school as their bodies are undergoing huge hormone shifts and resolves once they hit their growth spurt. They can be reluctant to go to swim parties and stop enjoying shopping for clothes.

These years can be hard. They have a bombardment of emotions and hormones, and the extra weight can make their self-esteem plummet. The best thing you can do is tell them it's normal; it's God's way of preparing the body for the changes to come. Encourage them to be active. Do sports together with them. My youngest daughter and I started taking boxing classes together. It's a great exercise and has given us some quality time together.

There is no magic size or body type that can ever make you feel confident, secure, and perfect. I've been there, and it never came close to filling the void I was desperately trying to fill. Someone will always be taller, shorter, toner, or younger than you.

The real answer is to find peace. Not the temporary peace we can find working out at the gym, but the peace that we can only attain through looking at ourselves through God's eyes. Peace that God made us perfect, inside and out. It is critical to really let this belief permeate into our hearts and souls. Only then can we offer it to our children. Some of us who have been hurt by infidelity or victims of pornography addiction will have to look daily for God to restore our hearts to his truth and his image of us. The most attractive feature a woman can have is confidence, but more than that, the unsurpassed knowledge of beauty that comes from knowing you are created perfectly by God.

As my parents got older and the kids were in college or busy in high school doing their own things, I notice that my parents were missing them. We instituted a family dinner night. It was amazing how hard it was to pick one night that worked for all of the kids. They had jobs or activities all over the board. But it was important to me to keep these generations connected, so we made it work. Not perfectly at times, but it all worked out. Teaching my children to honor their grandparents and being sensitive their needs was important. My children's lives were getting busier, but my parent's lives were slowing down. Teenagers, who sometimes only focus on themselves, need to be reminded from time to time to see the needs of others.

I have dubbed the teenage years the "selfish years." Although that has a negative connotation, it is a critical stage of their development into adulthood. Teenagers are forming their own beliefs and evaluating the ones they were brought up with. This takes a bit of introspection. They figure out what they know is true, and test the things they are unsure of. Because I understand this process, I take their self-absorption with a grain of salt. At times, though, I do feel like I need to help them take their eyes off themselves and see the people and world around them.

I sometimes have to tell my oldest daughter when she feels crushed from the world beating her down to be grateful. Take your eyes off yourself, and do something for someone else. Doing this gets the focus off ourselves and all the injustices that we feel are happening to us. I tell her to make a list. I tell her this because I have had to make a regular practice of this myself. Every night I would call her, and she would have to tell me three things from her list that she was grateful for.

The other night before I went to bed, I was frustrated. I was talking things over with God. He broke through my self-pity and told me he would give me ten things tomorrow to be grateful for. I faced my challenges that day with a lighter spirit. Throughout that day I was amazed at what God showed me. This day that I had been dreading with a heavy heart was amazing. I got my ten things. And God proved his point. He gives us blessings every day. We just have to take our eyes off ourselves long enough to see them.

With teenagers, we have the opportunity to say, "God loves you so much," to our teenagers. God will never leave you. God had a purpose for you. You are of great worth to God. Do you know how I know that? Because that's how I feel about you, and if I feel that way about you, how much more does God feel about you?

With every word, look, thought, or action, we have the opportunity and responsibility to lift our kids to God's level and standard. We have the opportunity and responsibility to help them glimpse what God expects from them, as well as for them. We have the opportunity and responsibility to see each moment as a turning point, a life lesson, and a teachable moment. It is how we use these opportunities that we can choose to glorify God. This will change our lives as we respond in obedience to God, and it will change our children's lives.

When my teenagers share with me about a struggle or experience they are having, I have an opportunity and responsibility to point them to God. Sometimes it takes the form of encouragement, discernment, guidance, or just listening and praying silently. This has changed my perspective on raising teenagers. What a purpose it gave me to wake up and know that I have a chance to make a difference today.

Things that Go Bump in the Night

People always talk about spiritual warfare. How the Devil and his demons are fighting a battle on earth to steal away God's people and ruin their lives. I always believed in the Devil, but I was never one of those who put much thought into him. I guess I felt I was untouchable, and some of the stories people told seemed so out there. But the Devil is real. I know, and I believe now because he was in my house.

It happened a few years ago. My youngest daughter was having nightmares every night. She would wake up crying and so scared. She would tell me a man was in her room. At first I brushed it off. But as the days turned to weeks, I grew concerned. I asked her what he looked like. She said he was standing in her room just staring at her, and he was dressed all in dark with a black hat on. I grew concerned, as any mom would, that someone was scaring or hurting her. I asked her about her teachers, her friends' dads, and every male role model I could think of. I was going to go to the school and tell them that I thought something was happening at the school. But that night after another nightmare, and I had tucked my daughter back into bed, I picked up a book in my room. The book was about a woman going through a hard time. And then I couldn't believe what I was reading. She said she had nightmares, and when she woke, she saw a dark man standing in her room. It happened to her every night, and it was a demonic man. I immediately sat up and yelled, "Satan get out! Get away from my little girl, in the name of Jesus." I prayed and spoke out loud, telling him to go back to hell. The next night my daughter did not wake up with her nightmare. The following morning, she rushed into my room and said the man was gone!

I never believed, but Satan is real. I tell you this because I want you to know that he is real. The things we do in our life, the sin that we let in, leave footholds for Satan to torment us. Sometimes we open the door for our children, our spouse, or other loved ones. I truly believe God orchestrated me to pick up that book that night. I knew immediately what I was to do. As crazy and far-fetched as it sounds, I want you to know the Devil is real.

They call it the net, the web, for a reason. There are myriad ways to get caught or trapped with it. Our children are not exempt from this. In fact, they are targeted.

My husband was a computer programmer. We had a house full of computers. We were very aware of the dangers on the Internet. We had rules, we checked the history logs, and we kept the computers out in the open, not in their bedrooms. We were diligent about telling the children not to give out their names or any personal information. You don't communicate with people you don't know. We had our bases covered, and our kids protected, right? I wish the story ended there, but sometimes trouble comes like a thief in the night.

My oldest daughter is a nurturer. When she loves, she loves with her whole heart. If she sees someone hurting, she wants to help. When she was a freshman in high school, she heard rumors that a girl in her class had just lost her boyfriend to suicide. She didn't know this girl but approached her and asked if she could do anything. The girl became her friend on Myspace.

My daughter posted a comment on this girls Myspace page, and shortly after, a friend of this new girl posted to my daughter. He said he was the best friend of the boy who had killed himself, and he could use someone to talk to. My daughter asked this girl if she knew him. She said yes, so my daughter friended him. My daughter listened and comforted him, and their friendship grew. They were known to talk on the phone for hours.

Around then, my daughter's personality began to change. My life of the party, full of energy girl became withdrawn and mean-spirited. I remember wondering what happened to my daughter, and who is this girl?

One day I received a phone call from the boy she had become friends with. He asked where my daughter was. I thought it was odd. When I hung up the phone, my younger children told me that he had been calling them and asking them the same questions. A red flag went up. I started asking my daughter about him. Did she hang out with him at school; was he part of her friend circle? She said he went to a different high school, and she had never met him in person; she just talked to him on the phone. A day or two after this, his dad took a temporary job in New York and he went with him for part of the school year.

Packages started coming in the mail from New York, including expensive phones and stuffed animals for my younger children. I didn't know this at the time as they were going to my ex-husband's house. I told my daughter we needed to meet him, and I invited him over. At the last minute he would always have an emergency come up and could not join us. I was suspicious when he said his mom had been drinking and was in a terrible car accident. I had a feeling deep in my gut that something was up, so I looked it up in the newspaper. There was an accident that matched that description, so I dismissed my gut feelings.

You see, at this time I was so caught up in my own life drama and the fallout of divorce that I was functioning but not on all cylinders. I was in survival mode. I was broken. I had turned my whole world upside down and I was lost. Every day I felt like I was spinning plates, running from plate to plate frantically trying to keep them spinning without shattering to the ground. I was so caught up in my own emotions, and the fog in my head kept my focus on me, while my daughter was suffering and getting in over her head.

This boy started posting pictures taken from my daughter's Myspace page onto his page, saying they were boyfriend and girlfriend. My daughter began to feel like something wasn't right. He had become possessive and controlling. She told him to stop, deleted him from her Myspace page, and told him their friendship was over. He told her he would kill himself. My daughter was distraught. We called the police. I dug through the empty boxes that he had sent to my daughter and gave the police his address. The police called back. There was no building at that address in New York, just the burned remains of a building. The police told me the worst news ever. We had an Internet predator.

Somehow, God jarred me to my senses. I still didn't know what to do, but I prayed with such intensity that God put my head and feet in motion. The police seized all the computers at my ex-husband's house and sifted through everything. What they found would make any mother cry. After checking all the IP addresses, we found out that this man was pretending to be at least three different people. One was the boy who originally killed himself, one was the best friend who friended my daughter, and the third was a girl that he had introduced to the circle of friends. They profiled this man as being in his forties with a huge network of victims.

I got on task. How many other girls were falling prey to this predator at this very minute? I called the high school where this boy said he went to school. No record of him ever. No record of the boy who supposedly killed himself. I asked the parents of my daughter's friends who also become friends with this boy if they had ever met him. They all said yes. I had to specifically ask if they had seen him in person. They said, "Well no, but we saw his picture on his Myspace page." That is not the same! This picture, the police told me later, was taken from an Abercrombie ad.

In the end, the police were not able to track down this Internet predator. I need to impress on you that these men are geniuses. They know how to bounce Internet

IPs so they cannot be traced. They can see your child's weakness and use that to trap them. They are capable of brainwashing and turning your sweet child into a monster. They will cover their tracks just like he did all the way from New York, watching the news for an alibi for him to not show up for dinner.

By the time this was all uncovered, I barely recognized my daughter. I remember trying to talk with her, but it was like she was empty and void of any emotion. Honestly, I didn't know what to do. So I did the only thing I could do. I got down on my knees and prayed. I kept thinking, *This doesn't happen in my world. This is not possible.* But there I was. God gave me the strength and wisdom to take it one day at a time. I remember thinking God promises to provide manna, not for the month nor the week, but one day at a time.

Sitting on my bed with this teenager who barely resembled my daughter, I told her that she was in a deep, dark pit. I loved her, and I could not leave her there. I was going to pull her out. I took her out of school and enrolled her in an online high school. I told her that she had a right to a childhood, and if she wouldn't fight for it, I would. Moms don't give up on their child—ever. She came to work with me or went to work with her dad. She took online courses for her sophomore year. She let go of friends who were not good for her. I did not know if I would ever see my beautiful daughter restored to her old self, but I trusted God to direct my ways. With each day, I saw a piece of my daughter return. She was kind to her siblings again, and she smiled. Two weeks later she threw her arms around me and said, "Thank you for saving me." Two weeks!

I debated whether to share this story with you. It seems hard to express how dark of a time this was for all of us, and part of me does not want to revisit it. As I asked God for discernment, I felt like it was a story that needed to be told. Life happens. I am not ashamed of where I was at the time that caused me to miss so many things, but my heart is still so sad about it. If there were do overs, I would sign up. Thankfully, we do have Jesus's grace and mercy for us, and that can wash away all our shame. We can all be fooled by the Devil. He is, after all, the great deceiver. He hunts and tries to destroy God's people. Don't let him destroy your children. Fight for them. My daughter and I are so incredibly close now. The Devil does not stand a chance at getting a foothold between us, and my daughter knows I will never give up on her. Nor will her heavenly Father.

Letting God Handle the Little Things, and the Big

It's a mother's natural instinct to protect her young. I know I could never stab someone or shoot someone, but I also know if someone was torturing or killing my child, I could easily do so. This scares me on some level. Our protection mode, if left unchecked, has the potential to hurt our children. Sometimes we let our fears dictate our actions. We hear some story on TV, and a great fear swells within us. What if that happened to my child?

As much as we love our children, God's love is infinitely bigger. We need to do everything we can to protect our children and then place them in God's hands to handle the rest.

I was lucky I learned this early in my mothering. When my second child was born, she had a kidney problem. It went undetected for two months and then she got really sick. She had to endure numerous horrible tests. She was so little but so strong; it took four adults to tie her down and strap her head to a board. My heart broke to watch my child undergo these tests. Her eyes pierced my very soul, crying out for me to save her. I was so shaken by watching my child suffer. I felt like she looked at me and said, "Mom, why won't you make them stop." I often prayed several times a day. "Lord, give me strength, give me courage, and help me be strong. Help them find the problem soon." It was so hard because on the outside, my daughter looked perfect. She had rolls of baby fat and was the picture of a healthy baby. Sometimes I was even fooled and thought it was all a mistake.

At six months, my baby had surgery. They told me the surgery would last nine hours. After they took from me, I didn't know how I was going to sit and wait for nine long hours. A couple hours into the surgery God found me.

"Do you love your child?"

"With all my heart," I replied.

"As deep as your love for her is, mine is immeasurably deeper. This child belongs to me. She is gift I entrusted you with. Can you release her into my hands? Can you trust me to do what's best for her?"

A lump formed in my throat and drove me to my knees. I had never thought of her as God's. I knew in my heart she was safer in his hands than in mine. As I released her, a peace washed over me. The surgery was done in six hours. Everything went better than they had planned. As the weeks followed in the hospital, I was constantly aware of the grace and blessing God had given me.

We were in a large teaching hospital, so all the babies with kidney problems shared one big room separated only by curtains. I felt guilty that my baby was by far the healthiest one there. I would hear mothers sobbing throughout the night. I am ashamed to say now that I was tired, frustrated, and irritated by the intense sadness and grief all around me. There came a moment, finally, that thumped me between the eyeballs, giving me an aha moment. All the doctors and nurses loved to come and see my daughter. They stopped in often throughout the day. I finally realized why. My baby was going to go home. She was going to grow up, run, play, get her heart broken by a boy, get married, and have babies of her own. Most of the other babies would not get that chance. I thanked God that night and every night after that he entrusted my little girl to me.

At the beginning of the school year, when my son started kindergarten, they did an eye test on all the kids. The school nurse called me and said, "You have to get your son glasses immediately. He can't see at all! He missed everything on the eye chart."

I was rather surprised and wondered, *How could I have missed this?* Self-doubt crept into my heart, mixed with feelings of falling short as a mom. After a few moments of panic, I knew there had to be some logical explanation for this.

I ended up taking him to his pediatrician who confirmed what I suspected. The school had given him the eye chart test using letters. My son's eyes were fine; he just didn't know his letters! I wonder how many times we do that with our kids. Fill ourselves with self-doubt and worry without stepping back and looking at the big picture.

One of the best things we can do for our children is to pray for them. When they are little, we think we can keep them safe. We can protect them. A wise mom knows there are dangers lurking out there, but instead of living in fear of them, a wise mom protects what she can and asks for protection from God for what she can't.

When I was a little girl and people asked me what I wanted to when I grew up, I would always say, "A mommy." When all the other kids said they wanted to be a teacher, nurse, or ballerina, I wanted to be a mom. It was something so deep inside me that my greatest fear was that I would not live long enough to be one.

Imagine my heartbreak after I was married, tried to get pregnant, and could not. My struggle with infertility was nothing compared to the heartache many other women have gone through, but it was extremely scary and painful for me. I was a young, modest girl, and the numerous fertility tests left me feeling violated.

I vacillated between feeling like my body was a failure and trusting that God would have my back no matter what happened. After a million fertility tests, I was put on a fertility drug, and two months later, I was pregnant. Not everyone's story is so easy. My heart breaks for women who endure months of fertility treatments without any baby. I realize that God could have said no to me. He could have had other plans for my life. I am so humbled that he fulfilled the desires of my heart.

Not all pregnancies have a happy ending. I suffered two miscarriages. They were heart breaking. From the moment you find out you are pregnant, your whole life changes. That baby becomes a part of your future. You picture your life differently, and you fall madly in love with that picture. The second time I miscarried, I was four months pregnant, and the baby's heart stopped beating. I had no other symptoms, and my body still thought I was pregnant. I went home to wait for the inevitable. Why had this happened? I was mad at God. I felt like I was being punished, and I was so incredibly sad. I had a great Christian doctor who took me in his office and told me, "God loves you. It is nothing you did or could have done. God has many babies planned for you. Just not this one." At the time, I just wanted this one. I was heartbroken. As I look back now, I see that God is a restorer of dreams as well as people. If I had not lost that baby, I would never have had my middle child. I got pregnant two months after that miscarriage, and God blessed me with the most amazing, compassionate child. God had taken something bad and used it for his good. I couldn't see it then, but years later, the reality of this revelation deepened my trust in God.

That pregnancy was not smooth sailing, though. Three months into the pregnancy, I got the flu. Not the twenty-four-hour flu; not even the ten-day flu. I had true influenza that lasted for thirty days. I spiked a 104 degree fever for twenty-two days. I lay in ice water in the bathtub but could not get my fever down. My doctor told me I would probably lose the baby. On my knees in my closet, I begged to God, begging like I have never done before or since. I tried bargaining between fits of anger and complete brokenness.

When the flu was gone and the pregnancy survived, I knew it was not for me that this baby lived. It wasn't because I prayed the right prayer, or I deserved to have this baby. It was because God had a plan. He had special plans for my little boy. Today, my son is in college. He is an assistant youth pastor, and his desire is to be a Christian counselor and set up a home for boys.

WHEN TROUBLE COMES

"In this world you will have trouble" (John 16:33). I love that verse. It's one of my favorites. If the verse had said, "If trouble comes," that would change everything. "If" implies that there is a chance that trouble will not come. If, implies that possibly "if" I was a better Christian, prayed more, or hadn't made past mistakes that I could surpass any trouble or suffering. "If" I was good enough, or "if" I hadn't done that one thing, I wouldn't be faced with this trouble. "If" makes me feel guilty and that I was totally in control to avoid this. But the verse says "when." God knows that our lives will contain trouble at some time. Because trouble will come, it makes me realize it's not the trouble itself that is the problem. It's how we choose to overcome trouble and the process of getting through it.

The best defense against trouble is to lay a strong foundation. With your children it means starting when they are very young. My husband and I always told our children that it was important to tell the truth. We would always have their backs as long as we knew what we were up against. One of the most important things I wanted my children to learn was that all of us make mistakes. None of us are perfect. Making a mistake is not a sign of weakness. Not owning up to it is. It takes great character and humility to admit when we are wrong. Having a contrite heart was a cornerstone in my parenting beliefs. Taking ownership of our mistakes allows us a chance to reconcile, say I'm sorry, right the wrong, and learn from it. Thinking you will never make a mistake is a symptom of pride. Failure can be a source of blessing, humbling you and giving you empathy for other people in their weaknesses. But most important, failure heightens our dependence on God.

I have reaped the benefits of laying this strong foundation. A side benefit to allowing my children to make mistakes has been that they have felt safe to tell me things. They felt safe to come to me when they have gotten into something over their heads. I always told my teenagers, "If you are ever in over your head, call me to come and get you. No questions asked."

I got a call from my oldest son one day. He was out with some friends. He said, "Mom, I think I'm in trouble. I don't know what to do." The buddies he was with decided to siphon gas from a neighbor's car. My son told them to let him out down the street. That still, small voice was telling him it was not okay. And then he called me. I went and picked him up. By then we realized the boys had tried to siphon gas from an off-duty police officer! We drove up to the house, and my son faced his mistake head on and talked with the officer. Although the situation was bad, the outcome was a great opportunity for humility, grace, and owning up to your mistakes.

Your children learn to say they are sorry and own up to their mistakes by watching you. One of the worst things you can do is pretend to be perfect. First, they will eventually grow up and realize you're not, and second, they may see you as perfect and an immeasurable standard that they can't live up to.

God can use all things for good. Problems are not random mistakes. They are hand-tailored blessings designed for your benefit and growth. Embrace all circumstances that God allows in your life, trusting he will bring good out of them.

Single Moms

Being a single mom is hard. There was a reason God's plan for procreation took a male and female. I read in the Bible that God hates divorce. It took me some time to realize that God doesn't hate me because I am divorced. He hates what it does to people he loves. It is devastating and leaves broken hearts, abandoned dreams, and broken children. If I'm quite honest with myself, I hate that, too. But life is messy, and even our best intentions and dreams can fall apart.

In today's world, communities and churches embrace, nurture, and provide encouragement for single moms. And that is a blessing. However, the stigma of being a divorced woman can linger deep down in us. The shame and the rejection we feel can take root in our hearts and prevent us from receiving the healing God so wants for us and the courage to face the unknown path we are now on.

Our God is an all-knowing God. He is omnipresent and omniscient. One day it dawned on me. God knew I was going to be right here, divorced and broken. I don't know why that gave me so much peace. Perhaps it was because God loved me before the divorce, knowing I would be found here. Therefore, he loves me now. Also, I took great comfort in the fact that God knew exactly where I was going to go from here even if I didn't.

I was driving in my car one day, feeling broken and afraid, and God spoke to me. "I know the plans I have for you" (Jeremiah 29:11). I wept. The almighty, all-powerful Lord had a plan to restore me, and he already knew the outcome. His plans for me were good and full of blessings. That was the greatest comfort I could imagine. Sometimes the happiest endings are not the ones you keep longing for but something you absolutely cannot see from where you are.

God's grace will carry you through even the darkest days. After my divorce, my youngest daughter was really struggling. I watched this beautiful, full of life child withdraw and become sad. I struggled to reach her and comfort her and make any headway. I was sitting at her school gym for her chorus concert with a hundred other parents. The kids were all lining up on stage to take their places, and something amazing happened. All the sudden I was in an enormous theater. The lights were all down except a spotlight on a young woman standing on stage. That young woman was my daughter. I don't know if she was singing or talking or why she was up there, but she was beautiful and smiling. I knew in that very moment that God had given me a vision, a glimpse to reassure me that my daughter was going to be just fine. I so needed that message from God. I have never before or since had any kind of visions. But I am certain that God's grace reached down to touch a mother's heart and give her hope and peace.

Being a single mom can have great rewards. I know that sounds crazy, especially if you find yourself facing it. But God can use all things for his good, and single moms will find nuggets of gold in their coal.

One of the blessings will be the bonding that can happen with your kids and you. With five kids I needed their help. They were a necessary commodity in my overstretched, overworked life. I told them I needed them, and they were important. This gave them a purpose and a job in an otherwise turbulent time in their life.

While I was cooking dinner, one of the older kids would help the younger ones with homework. Another would play or read stories, and one would rock the baby. I was not afraid to delegate, especially on math homework. By the time my children reached the fourth grade, I was no longer an asset to them in this department anyway.

Everyone's needs were being met by being cared for or by the importance of caring for someone else. I made a chart for bedtime reading. The older kids took turns reading their younger sister or brother a bedtime story. At the time, this allowed me to be where I was really needed at the moment, to tend to a sick child, or to talk with someone about something that was bothering them.

As my children grew, they cooked dinner, did the grocery shopping for me, and continued to take care of each other's needs.

The greatest gift from this practice came when my children grew up. The first people my children turn to for help or encouragement is each other. When life presses down on them about friends, relationships, or heartbreaks, they reach out and lean on each other. My children knew when they were little that they were a vital piece in our family puzzle. Together we could do anything, and they could always count on each other to be there for them.

I wanted my children to know their dad and to love him without limits and without my input of the negative feelings I had. It was hard at times to defend him, to build him up. But I also knew I had to remind my children that we are all broken, and God loves him very much. I wanted to remind them and point them to the wonderful attributes their dad had. I wanted them to be free to see all the wonderful pieces of their dad. I felt like my children deserved to develop their own beliefs and relationships based on their experiences with their dad. I knew they would face the same things I had, but I needed them to discover them on their own. Now, as young adults, they bring their wounded hearts to me, and we can really talk about these things.

You cannot be a single mom without sacrifice. You sacrifice dinners out and possibly the better job, but the one that would take you away from your children. I felt that I was entrusted with five children to nurture and raise to God-loving adults. That meant they came first.

God became the man in my life. His promise to never leave or forsake me was everything to me. I talked with God about a problem with my kids like it was just the two of us sitting at the kitchen table. I went to God with work problems, with relationship problems, and with money problems. There were so many times that my rent would be due the next day and I had no idea how I was going to come up with it. I prayed and trusted God constantly, but deep down I still had this doubt that God's promise to provide for me would be real. And time after time, God came through for me. He never got mad at me for my doubt but, instead, was exactly who he promised to be. Sometimes it showed up through a big tip a customer left. Sometimes it was a call out of the blue for an art piece. Sometimes it meant humbling me and letting go of my pride to let someone else help me. God put people in my path to give me gifts, like movie tickets or gift cards for the holidays.

There is a folk song my aunt and uncle sing called "Desert Pete." It is a story about a man in the desert who comes upon a water pump. There is small jar of water with a note attached saying, "It takes all this water to prime the pump. Don't be tempted to quench your thirst. You must have faith and believe." I have found myself at the pump many times. It seems like I journey from pump to pump. You would think after having faith to use that water to prime the pump once, every time after would be easy. But it never works like that. I wonder, *What if it doesn't work this time? What if my luck runs out? What if it's not God's plan?* But God promises to fill our needs. It would sure be nice if God just provided for me in a lump sum. Imagine how nice it would be to not have to worry for a couple months. But God doesn't work like that. He provides manna for one day at a time. We must have faith and believe that God will be who he says he is. I realized all this through the process of being a single mom. As my pastor says, "The deep end exposes our need for God like the shallow end never can."

As a single mom, I desperately needed God. Not just the magic potion, fairy dust kind of God, but the real, live, "I can't do this on my own" God. I faced situations and decisions that I didn't have the strength or knowledge to figure out. God was not only in my thoughts constantly; he walked right beside me. I was a broken woman, trying to raise God-loving children, and I made my share of messes along the way. But our God is a patient God. When I could not stand on my own anymore, I got on my knees and asked forgiveness and guidance. God's grace picked me up and set me on my path again.

Servant Heart

Sometimes the demands of raising a family can overwhelm us, make us resentful and even angry at others. When I load the dishwasher for the second time that day and wipe my chapped hands from washing pots and pans, I feel like Cinderella waiting to be swept away to the ball. But it is not Cinderella we should be looking to but Jesus. Jesus is an amazing example of a servant heart. He came to serve. He did so with a joyful heart. I'm sure he didn't say, "Oh, man, great. Another person who needs to be healed. What about me? I was right in the middle of something for myself. Can't somebody else do it?" Whenever I feel stressed, taken advantage of, or underappreciated, I have learned to stop and turn my eyes to Jesus. These blessings you have entrusted me with are pure joy. I am so thankful I have a healthy body to be able to take care of them.

When we serve our family with a joyful heart, our tasks seem easier, the burdens lighter, and the resentments melt away. They are replaced with a grateful happy heart. Of course, sometimes in the midst of feeling like the demands are never ending, I can't always flip a switch and feel the warm fuzzies toward my fellow human. At these times, I have learned one simple solution to change my heart. It's not a vacation, a spa day, or eating a gallon of my favorite ice cream. After any of those things, I would have to return to the same situation I was running from. The solution is to pray for my children or others that have wronged me. It is tempting to pray they will pick up their clothes, unload the dishwasher without being asked, or maybe even feed the dog. Maybe if God would just whip them into shape. But instead, I bite my tongue and pray for their protection, their happiness, their walk, their strength, and their health. This always leads to my incredible thankfulness that they are in my life. I thank God I have them to love. The result is not that they have changed, but I have. My heart has changed. It is pure joy to serve my family.

One of my greatest joys of motherhood was nursing my baby. Anyone who has nursed knows that it is rarely convenient. You have to stop whatever you are doing, wherever you are, and feed your baby. I loved being the only one who could do this for my baby. I could have given my baby a bottle (although none of my children would ever accept one), but I relished this time. I am a doer. I usually do five things at once, but stopping to sit and spend that time with my precious little one was a gift.

Having a servant heart through the years built trust and made my kids feel safe. They knew Mom would be there no matter what. I got a call well after midnight on night from my teenage son. His car had started overheating, so he put antifreeze in it. It started smoking and died on the freeway. He and his friend pushed the car to safety, and he called me. While talking to him, we realized he had put the antifreeze in the oil compartment. I grabbed my keys and headed to help him. Even at that hour in Phoenix, it was well over 100 degrees. The heat coming off the blacktop under the car burned our skin. We could not for the life of us get that oil pan cap off to drain the oil. We took turns for a couple hours, scorching our bodies under that car. At one point I just started laughing, a real belly laugh that brought tears to my eyes. "Only you, Mom, could have a smile on your face at a time like this. I love that about you," my son said. The truth is I learned a long time ago that you have to put things in perspective. My son had called me because his car broke down. He wasn't in an accident. I knew eventually (although I was struggling at the present time) that I could put his car back together. I could not have fixed my broken son.

Eventually, he called a friend's dad to help him get the cap off. My son changed, drained, and refilled his oil three times in a row. The car was fine. A couple days later, he told me he felt so stupid for making that mistake in the first place. I gently reminded him of the blessing. He will never have to pay someone else to change his oil again because now he is an expert! Sometimes when we make a mistake, we can blame someone else or ourselves, but rarely is there not a positive lesson in our mistakes. A mom after God's own heart helps her child see the benefit of a mistake.

After I got divorced, I had a hard time getting a job. I had spent twenty plus years being a stay-at-home mom and homemaker. My last experience was being a waitress. *Hey,* I thought, *I'm good at stepping and fetching. I can do that.* One of the waitress jobs I had was at resort, taking drinks to families swimming and laughing at the pool. I remember the horrible gut-wrenching feeling I had at this job. I would walk around and see moms and kids on vacation, having fun and playing. And I would think in heartbroken anger, *That should be me. I should be the one being waited on and playing with my kids.* I left work most days teary-eyed and broken in self-pity. It was almost painful to go to work. I dreaded it. It was a constant reminder that I was nothing anymore. Thank goodness God didn't leave me there, drowning in self-pity. One morning he spoke to me as clear as day. "I know you are hurting. I know your life is not as you planned. But remember, even my own Son came to serve. When you serve others, think of my Son, and think of serving me." That pep talk from God exposed my wounded heart but restored my God-honoring character.

I have had other serving jobs since, and part of me loves it. It is my pleasure to serve. And on those rough nights when people are impatient and rude, I try to remember the Jesus came to serve others. Now my prayer is that God will use me to touch one person's life. More often than not, one of my customers touches mine. Many people would ask me, "You're just a waitress?" I hope I am setting an example to my children that it takes a very humble, unselfish heart to serve others. Jesus came to serve; he washed his disciples' feet. If it's not beneath him, surely it is not beneath us to serve others.

Growing up, my parents were very good at teaching us to serve others and help those in need. My dad owned trailer parks and trailers, and we spent many weekends helping people there. We brought them food and bags of oranges and grapefruit. If my dad knew they had children about my size, he would ask me if I had some clothes to give them. At times, Dad would buy a window air conditioner for a family. If someone was struggling to pay rent, he would let it slide. My dad had the best servant heart. I grew up knowing I was very blessed. I grew up knowing how great it feels to help someone else. In fact, it feels much better to give than receive.

Money was tight after I got divorced. I could barely pay my bills and, in truth, had to borrow money from my sister or my dad to do even that. The first year I was divorced, I became very anxious and depressed as Christmas approached. My younger children still believed in Santa, and I knew there was no money to buy them anything. I didn't know how I was going to put any presents under the tree. I was a manager at a restaurant at the time, and my staff would ask me what Santa was bringing my kids. They were so excited to hear all the children's dreams and wishes. But inside I was so sad. I felt hopeless that I could pull it off. I made my kids gifts as I had always done, using things I had around the house. I gave my son my cell phone because that was all he wanted. A few years prior, I bought him a Power Ranger play flip phone and put it in a T-Mobile box, and it made him cry. So my heart wanted him to have my phone. I had a decorative pine tree that was in my boys' room, and I pulled that out and decorated it with all the Christmas tree ornaments. I was embarrassed by my tree until I heard my daughter's best friend on the phone with her mom asking why they couldn't have a cute, little Charlie Brown tree. My paradigm shifted, and I wasn't so sad anymore.

As Christmas Eve came to a close, we headed home from church and the evening spent with my parents. As we approached the house, I noticed something odd. Lining the stone walkway up to my house were all these wrapped gifts. And right by the door was a twelve-foot, fresh-cut Christmas tree with a beautiful angel on top. The kids jumped out of the car and ran down the walkway. "This one has my name on it! It's from Santa," they called one by one. I began to cry, but not out of joy or happiness. They were tears of shame and embarrassment.

When I looked over at my oldest daughter, her eyes were moist, too, but not for the same reason as mine. "Mom, who did this?" she asked. "I can't believe someone would love you so much to do this." I really had no idea. My children had more presents than they ever had! And it was everything they had asked for from Santa. I found out later all my employees had played Santa's little elves. I was deeply touched, but my pride robbed me of the true blessing. I guess on some level I wanted to the hero. I wanted the joy of giving so much that I missed the grace of receiving.

Fast-forward eight years. My oldest son, a youth pastor, was talking with his youth group and asked them what was the best Christmas they ever had. After they had all answered, they said, "You grew up with four siblings; you must have had some great Christmases." My son proceeded to tell them about the Christmas that gifts lined our walkway. That was my son's favorite Christmas? Not the year he got his bicycle or the year he got drum set? The kids asked if they could do something like that because it was amazing. When my son told me this, my shame melted away, and I understood for the first time the beauty of that Christmas. My children received the greatest gift, one that I could never have bought if I had all the money in the world. That simple act of kindness is being paid forward in the lives of the people it touched and the story as it is passed down and retold.

The People God Puts in Your Path

I have a very big secret. It's huge! Well, it's not so much a secret, at least not to moms. All moms know this secret. I wish everyone knew. It seems basic, and it's unimaginable that everyone doesn't know. After all, everyone has heard the old saying, "The way to a man's heart is through his stomach." Does anyone ever wonder the way to a woman's heart? Here it is. If you want to be endeared to a woman forever, love her children. We can complain and go on and on about our children's misbehavior or poor judgments, but woe is the fool who talks bad about our kids! There is a bond between a mother and her child, a protective line that cannot be crossed. Like a mama bear protecting her cubs, we will risk our own security and status to defend them.

The people who endear our children to them hold very sacred and special places in our hearts. They are more precious to us than rubies. They are the people God has put in our paths to come alongside us and help us. They are there to smooth out the rough edges when we are exhausted and out of steam. They are there to pick up where we have left off when the physical demands take their toll on us. They are there to teach our children things and expose them to new ideas and adventures out of our range of expertise or experience. They are many hands and hearts, working together to grow happy, healthy, God-loving children.

I'm not sure my children know how blessed they are to have the grandparents they do. But I do. My parents have been instrumental in developing my children's character and enriching their lives.

As a child, my parents would load the family up and take off on a road trip for the summer. Almost always we eventually ended up on our family's farm in Minnesota. I have camped in over forty-two of the United States. I have been to every national park and monument, big and small, in all those states. As soon as my kids were old enough to travel, my parents started taking them on these trips. It was not always easy for me to let my young children travel the country without me. I was scared and nervous to have them out of my protective, watchful eye. But my God was bigger than my fears, and I trusted him. I can't imagine if I hadn't placed my faith in God. Those trips were some of the best memories my children have. When my youngest son was in the fifth grade, he was asked to be in a geography bee. Everyone was so surprised at how much he knew about rivers, mountains, and national monuments. He simply told them, "I've been there."

I loved being pregnant. But with that came a constant companion: vomiting. It was so bad that I could barely function in the mornings. I would set out filled cereal bowls on the table the night before and fill sippy cups with milk and place them on a low shelf in the fridge so my son could pour them over their cereal in the morning as I supervised from the couch. A routine trip to the grocery store meant pulling over to the side of the road frequently so I could be sick. When I was pregnant with my fourth baby, my mother-in-law showed up at my door. She bagged up all my dirty laundry and took it to the Laundromat. She returned with fresh, clean, and neatly folded stacks of clothes. It was a blessing!

My mother-in-law took each of my children on a trip when they graduated sixth grade. They got to pick anywhere in the United States they would like to go. My oldest son went to Washington DC. My daughter, fitting to her personality, picked the Mall of America. Another one of my children picked Disney World, another Boston to see a Red Sox game, and my youngest daughter picked swimming with the dolphins in California. Those trips were memory makers for my children. They felt valued, precious, and loved.

My mother-in-law would often take my girls for overnights and to teach them to quilt and sew a project. My mother made memories with my children by making cut-out cookies with them. I have inherited her cookie-cutter collection of over a thousand cookie cutters. Someday I will pass these down to my children.

My father-in-law shared adventures with my kids, taking them fly fishing, four-wheeling, and camping in the bunkhouse. My kids looked forward to school breaks when they could head to northern Arizona to spend time with him. He was a woodworker and spent many hours helping the kids build whatever they wanted.

When my third child was two, he didn't talk much. Okay, he didn't really talk at all. The older two communicated with him in their own language of grunts and gestures. My mom was concerned that he wasn't talking. I laughed. My older daughter talked nonstop and enough for both of them! I was truly enjoying the peace and quiet. But my mom decided that he needed to come to "Grandma's School" to help him talk. He loved it! He would wait with the other kids at the bus stop with his backpack on, and once the school bus pulled away, he would yell, "Grandma's School!" And off he would go with my dad to spend the morning with Grandma.

My dad taught my children a lot. He was the first person they turned to for help with their car. My dad taught them how to change car parts and identify problems. This was a much-needed skill in our house! My dad taught my boys how to ride a bike and how to fix broken toys. My youngest boy was an early riser, very unlike the rest of our clan. When we went camping, my dad would get up before the sun rose and take walks with him. They would watch the sun come up over the ocean or look for treasures from the sea or animal tracks in the woods. By the time we all rose from our sleepy slumber, they would have had numerous adventures and experiences of God's beauty and creation. The moments that they shared together are dear to my heart. His patience was immeasurable, and his gentleness in instruction was what my kids remember the most.

My sister married later in life and did not have children. She told me that I have enough children for her to enjoy. She has been a huge blessing in my life.

She is my children's biggest cheerleader. She comes to every concert, play, and sports game my children are in. She can track my children down wherever they are. We have a joke in our family that if one of my children were ever abducted, we are to call my sister first because she can find them!

God placed good friends in my path as my children were growing up. They were friends with young children who I could share with and encourage on our journeys. Some of those friends have fallen by the wayside through the years. These people were my central support system and rooted in my life so deeply. I was so sad when things started drifting apart, and I tried to hold on for dear life. But God gently reminded me that they were in my path for a purpose and for a time. They were orchestrated by him. I found peace in letting them go, knowing that God was making room in my life for someone else to join me for the rest of the journey. I have one dear friend who is a constant in my life. I know she is my God-given gift, my encourager. She has been through the bitter and the sweet of my life and continues to this day to point me to Jesus.

I was lucky to find a man who learned to love God, someone who would pray with me for our children and help them navigate through life. I'm sure my dad was thrilled to hand his tools over to him, so he could help the kids with their cars. It wasn't always easy to let someone come alongside me with my children, but as he grows in the Lord, he is a blessing to me and my kids.

When I was going through my divorce, it was pretty rough on my oldest son. He turned to a youth pastor for help, guidance, and encouragement. The young man who touched my son so deeply and turned him to God has a special place in my heart. He did for him what I could not do at the time, and it made all the difference in the world.

Most tender to my heart was my children's great-grandmother. She was a godly woman. She had a servant heart, and she modeled to my children what it meant to be a virtuous woman. She was always giving, always doing for others, when she could have easily been the one receiving. She saw people's needs and reached out to them. She had a smile on her face no matter what was happening in her life. God was her strength. But the reason she has taken a special, sacred spot in my heart was how she loved my youngest son. She saw the best in everyone. She passed by the rough spots and saw the beauty. She saw that in my son. It touched my heart in the most dramatic way. I love my son so much, and it always broke my heart that he was misunderstood and not as openly loved and accepted by people in my life. But she loved him with all her heart. And in return, he loved her passionately. When she lay dying in the hospital, my son crawled upon the bed next her. After he left the room, he fell to the ground weeping. This is the woman who stole my heart, who touched so deeply the life of my son, who loved unconditionally.

Retreat to the Desert

Every mom needs to take time to recharge her batteries. At first I did this instinctively, but as my children grew older, I had to learn how to retreat. Jesus did this. He took time to be alone with God and recharge his batteries. He knew how important it was.

When my children were small, no matter how tired I was, I put them to bed and had some "me time." Bedtimes to me were very important. After bath and story time for the little ones, it was lights out. The older children had showers and reading quietly in their beds for a half hour. That gave me time to straighten up and clean the kitchen, which I always did. (It was a little trick my mom taught me. Don't wake up to yesterday's mess; tomorrow will have its own.) After that it was my time. I knew enough about myself to know I needed some time of quiet in my head. It was these times that God spoke to me. "Be still and know that I am God" (Psalm 46:10). God revealed things to me and straightened out my thoughts.

As my children got older, it was harder to have any downtime. Kids were up later or had jobs or dates that brought them home later. I noticed a mood shift in me.

I was frustrated and felt overburdened with people. It took me a while to realize that I was not getting my downtime anymore. I was a person who needed my alone time to debrief uninterrupted with God and my own thoughts.

Everyone has different ways to recharge their batteries. Maybe you need to get out of the house. Maybe you need coffee with a friend. As a mom, we give and give and give. If we don't take time to recharge our reserve, we can find ourselves running on empty with nothing else to give.

Letting Go

In the weeks before my son's wedding, we talked a lot of his future plans and God's desire for his life. One night he came into my room and said that right after the wedding, he and his new bride were moving to Nebraska. "You are the only person who could ask me to stay and I would," he said.

What could I say? I loved my son with all my heart. And although my heart was breaking at the time, I knew it was best for him. He was the oldest of five kids and had always been more of a dad than a brother to them. I knew he needed to bond with his wife, and it would be harder with all the family around. I also knew my son was praying and asking God's guidance. I swallowed the lump in my throat and presented the best smile I could muster. "I think it's a great idea!" In the weeks that followed, I was fine. Really fine. That is until the night of the rehearsal dinner. Nothing could have prepared me for the bombshell of emotions that hit me. And then it struck me. It wasn't that my son was moving away; it was that another woman had taken my place. She would be comforting him on a bad day; she would be taking care of him when he was sick. She would get to hear the, "I'm home," at the end of the day. I missed my position already.

I was so happy for him. He had picked a beautiful, godly wife who loved Jesus with all her heart. But at the same time, my arms ached to turn the clock back and hold my little boy all over again. At coffee a few days later, when I told my dearest friend how much I missed my son, she said, "Girl, you still have four more at home!" I don't think it matters how many kids you have. When one from your nest is missing, you feel a great loss. She gently reminded me that I had fulfilled God's great request of me. I had raised a God-honoring, loving son to manhood.

I miss my late night talks with my son. I miss feeling his arms around me. I don't get to talk to him or see him as much as I would like. But those things have been replaced with all the most beautiful things God is doing in and through his life. In a letter to my son, I told him I was so proud of the man he had become. When he was small, I felt like he was mine. As time went on, I grew to understand that he was not mine but God's and entrusted to me. He was mine to love, to teach, to enjoy, and to direct to Jesus. I will never forget the moment I realized that as much as I loved him, God loved him more. It was almost unimaginable. So many people asked if I felt like I was losing him now that he was getting married. The truth is no because he has always been and always will be God's. So my position didn't change. I'm his mom. I will always be here to support him, encourage him, and point him back to Jesus if necessary.

My child—who growing up said he should have been an only child because he needed quiet and alone time, who said it was too much responsibility to be an example to his younger siblings, my genius child who could have made fame and fortune—laid it all down when God called him to be a youth pastor. It puts a smile on my face to think of him spending 24/7 with young kids. God really has a sense of humor. But more important, God has a purpose and a plan for our lives.

Through the years, I have always kept a prayer journal. I'm not sure if it truly qualifies as a prayer journal, but it was a book where I poured my heart out to God. Sometimes they were just thoughts I wanted to share with him. Other times they were praises or petitions I was bringing before him. I had a section for each of my children.

Twenty years and twenty prayer books later, my oldest son was getting married. I sorted through old photos and books. I got lost in the memories of old notes and photographs, which is probably why I never pretend to sort through and throw things out! I came across my first prayer book and flipped to the section with my baby boy's photo on it. My little boy, all grown up now, was getting married next week. And then I see it. The memory comes flooding back to me.

My little boy is three years old. I'm tucking him in to bed for the night.

"Mommy, I love you so much. When I grow up, I am going to marry you." He throws his arms around me. I can smell that freshly bathed baby smell still clinging to that space between his neck and his ear.

I tell him I love him so much, but I'm already married to Daddy. But somewhere out there is a little girl who is growing up with her family. God had already picked her to be his wife. As we say our prayers, we pray for this little girl, wherever she is, that God will protect her and guide her and that she will love Jesus just like my little boy.

That night before I went to bed, I wrote in my book a special prayer to God for this little girl who would capture my son's heart. The memory brought tears to my eyes, and I have a huge lump in my throat. "So, God, is this that little girl you were watching over?" I thanked God for leading me to find this prayer at this time. I had completely forgotten about it. God fulfilled my prayer all those years ago. The woman my son was to be married to loved Jesus with all her heart. What a faithful God! I read this prayer from my journal at their wedding.

As my children grow up and move into adulthood, at times I find myself longing for my full house, with all the noise, commotion, and laughter that used to fill all the rooms. The emptiness echoes through my soul. Sometimes I find myself lost for a moment in time when I glance at a picture on the wall of my babies who are all grown up now.

Rewards of Grown-Up Kids

One of the misconceptions I had was that at some point, your mothering is over. I have learned that you never stop being a mom, no matter how old your children are. When you hear sirens you still worry. "Is my child okay?" When the phone rings at 2 a.m., you still pick it up and listen to your child's struggles in an unfair and broken world.

I'm not sure why I believed that one day my children would outgrow me, be too wise for me, or replace me with a spouse. The truth is I still run to my own parents for advice and comfort. Now more than ever, I appreciate their wisdom and experience, and I am eager to listen. My children have always been smarter than me, but they are not coming to me for my intellect. They are coming to me for wisdom, for life experience, for comfort, but most of all, to tap into my close relationship with Jesus.

It's a funny thing when we have poured our hearts and souls into our children for years and then see them as adults, bearing fruit as from our labor. It is the circle of blessings. The first people I want to go to with a problem or concern are my adult children. These children, who I have taught for years, are now teaching me and confirming my faith in a loving God.

My dad means the world to me. If I need advice on something, if I need help, or I just need to talk, I go to my dad. I began to worry about my dad. He was in his eighties and displaying some medical symptoms that concerned me. My brother was dying of cancer, and I could see the stress on my dad's face. That, coupled with the heartbreaking reality of eventual loss of my big brother, was weighing greatly on me. When I would see my dad, tears filled my eyes. When I would hug him good-bye, I would feel this gut-wrenching pain of wondering if it was the last time I would get to hug him. I was consumed with fear. It dug its ugly teeth into me and would not let go. I would cry out to God and tell him, "I can't lose my dad now. I'm not ready! I still need him! Do not take him from me." I lived in constant fear and anxiety, and panic became my ever-present companion. I finally shared my fears with my oldest son. His words cut through my self-obsessed pain and were like a torch filling all the dark corners of my soul. "Mom, you spend so much time worrying about losing him one day that you are missing the time now that you have with him."

As we talked, I realized that I had made my dad an idol in my life. Over and over, the Bible warns us about making idols in our life. Some people make idols of money, some of work, some of people. Mine was my dad. Our God is a very jealous God. I am reminded of the story of Abraham and his son Isaac. God told him if he loved him (God) that he needed to sacrifice his son to him. Abraham loved his son so much, so with tears in his eyes, he lifted his sword to kill his son. God stopped him in time. Point taken.

Talking with my son, I realized I was not trusting God with my dad. I was clutching him tightly in my hands and saying, "You can't have this!" My dad is eighty-four. I know a time will come when God will take him home. And I know I will not be ready to lose him ... ever. I will still need him. But my heavenly Father will be there for me. My son opened my eyes to this.

> Watch yourselves closely so that you do not forget the things your eyes have seen or let them slip from your heart as long as you live. Teach them to your children and to their children after them. (Deuteronomy 4:90)

Adoption

I wanted to include a chapter on adoption. Although none of my children were adopted, I was. When I was growing up, kids loved to tease me, saying, "Your mom didn't even want you. She gave you away."

It was a futile battle because I was so proud to be adopted. My retort was always, "No, your parents were stuck with you; mine picked me out!" And that is how I felt. I felt special, unique, very loved, and wanted.

When I was in the seventh grade, someone asked me, "When did you find out you were adopted?"

I was stumped. All I could reply was, "I don't know. I have just always known." I asked my mom that day when I got home when they had told me I was adopted. She told me from the day they brought me home. That's why it was just a part of me for as long as I could remember.

Having a child grow inside me and feeling utter love and attachment to that baby even before it was born touched my heart so deeply. The selflessness and sacrifice that giving up a baby means gripped me to the core. I finally understood the heart-wrenching decision that giving your baby up was.

When my first child was born, I marveled at how familiar his features were. I had never thought about genetics in the familial way before. I thought of my birth mother a lot in those early years while I was pregnant or had just brought home a new baby from the hospital. I wondered if I could have ever been that selfless. Could I have ever let my baby go even if it was the best thing for him or her? It bothered me on some level because I'm not sure I could have. My respect and admiration for the girl who showed unfathomable courage and selflessness grew to immeasurable bounds.

After my third child was born, on a trip to my home state, I went to the children's home where I was adopted. Part of me had to know if I had the same guts and integrity that my birth mother had. The other part of me needed to know for my children the medical history.

They presented me with my file, which included interviews and family history, and a photo of me taken in that very room. As I read through the file I was shocked to see that the description of my birth mother was describing me to a T. Not only her looks, but her talents, passions, and the mannerisms were all me! As I read more, I couldn't believe it, and I saw how God's hand had been working in my life from the very beginning. My young birth parents were Quakers. They were very God-loving. God placed me in a family that went to church every Sunday and loved God. My paternal grandfather loved animals. God placed me in a family where my father was a large-animal veterinarian. I could now see the thin strings of all these things working together. It allowed me to grow up in an environment that would nurture my innate being. It made me understand that generational sin can also be generational blessings.

Our Father

It is easy for me to believe how much God loves me, and his desire is to protect me and defend me. It is easy to believe that he will comfort me and encourage me. I know deep down in the depths of my soul that he will always be there for me. It is easy to believe that because my earthly father is just like that.

When I think of the word "father," it is a warm blanket wrapped around me on a cold night. It is safety and unconditional love. Unfortunately, not everyone has a father like that. It may be harder for them to believe that their heavenly Father offers us all that and so much more.

But he has written us a love letter filled with all those promises and more. Our love letter is the Bible. He declares we are his children. We are his heirs. He will discipline us and conform our hearts as any good parent would. He loves us too much to leave us where we are.

When I was in the fourth grade, I wanted a ball and jacks. My dad said no. It wasn't that they were expensive, so I couldn't understand why I could not have them. I wanted them so desperately that one day while I was at summer recreation, I took them. I tried to hide them from my parents, but one day, I left them lying on the ground, which was why my dad didn't want me to have them in the first place. I lied when I was discovered and told them they were a friend's. My lies unraveled, as they always do, and I soon had to confess that I had stolen them. I was forced to return them to the school and tell them what I had done. I was embarrassed and ashamed.

A couple years ago at Christmas, I got a small wrapped box from my dad. I opened it to find a ball and jacks. My dad chuckled and said, "I think you are ready for the responsibility of them now." I often wonder how many times we ask God for something and he says no, so we just go out and find a way to get it. When things turn disastrous, we try to hide it from him only to realize that we have been exposed. If we are smart, we ask for forgiveness, and God's grace wipes away the shame. Our heavenly Father knows what is best for us. His timing is always perfect. I keep that little box of jacks on my dresser as a constant reminder that God knows better than me when I am ready for things that I so desperately want.

Something that has always stuck with me is something that happened to me on a camping trip across country with my parents and two small children. We had stopped at a rest stop, and a young girl came up to my dad with some sob story and asking for money. My dad reached into his wallet, pulled out some bills, and handed them to her. My mom scolded my father, saying, "You know this is a scam, and she really doesn't need the money."

It was my dad's reply that stays with me to this day. He said, "It's not my job to decide if she is telling the truth or not, scamming me or not. It is my job to help someone in need." There have been many times that I have wanted to know that someone was deserving of it before I gave or did anything for them. But God requires us simply to act.

Quite often something will spur a memory and I'll ask the kids if they "remember when." Usually they say, "No, not really." The other night my son asked me, "Mom, how can you remember all these things?" I think the answer is because all these moments have been written on my heart, tattooed, etched, and forever imprinted there. I drank in every moment as if I was parched and desperate to fill this life with the five greatest gifts that God had given me.

One thing I am learning is to laugh more, be silly and enjoy the journey. I stopped majoring on the minors and am enjoying the ride.

Yesterday I had the privilege of hearing my twenty-two-month-old grandson sing "Jesus Loves Me." I wanted to stop everything and drink in the moment like a fine glass of wine. I want to kick my shoes off and sit and enjoy these very moments. They go by so fast. With my children, the days were long, but the years were short.

I have had the privilege to be a mom for not one child, not two children, not three children, not four children, but five children! I get to see five lives changed by God.

My children may never be famous, but for their children to know and love the Lord our God, and for them to teach their children, will be the most important thing. And then I will be able to feel that the purpose that God prepared in advance for me to do was accomplished.

Epilogue

Last week I shared my story with a complete stranger at church. I revealed all the broken bits of me that I keep neatly tucked away so no one can see. It was the naked truth of the heartbreak of raising children after divorce. I wondered after I shared with her if it was too much. I worried I had overstepped my bounds, and she would look at me through a new filter. The next week, this woman approached me with a big smile on her face. She thanked me with so much gratitude and genuine love. She told me that what I said helped her so much. I thought about it later and realized how much God desires us to share our experiences. We have this great opportunity to say, "God is faithful." My prayer for you is that you go forth in this world and share your story. It won't be like mine, but it will be like a beautiful, stained-glass window with many broken pieces coming together to make something beautiful again. May you proclaim God's goodness into the hearts of moms everywhere, and may his hand knit your family together into a lovely tapestry of his love.

Printed in Great Britain
by Amazon